Lichtheim, George
George Lukacs

GEORGE LUKÁCS

MODERN MASTERS

Already published

MODERN MASTERS

EDITED BY frank kermode

george
lukács

george lichtheim

NEW YORK | THE VIKING PRESS

In memoriam
Franz Borkenau
1900–1957

Published in 1970 in a hardbound
and a paperback edition
by The Viking Press, Inc.
625 Madison Avenue, New York, N.Y. 10022.

Distributed in Canada by
The Macmillan Company of Canada Limited.

SBN 670–33671–8 (hardbound)
SBN 670–01909–7 (paperbound)

Library of Congress catalog card number: 76–104146.

Printed in U.S.A.

PREFACE

This study of George Lukács is necessarily brief and selective. Its purpose is to facilitate access to an important writer most of whose work has appeared only in Hungarian or in German. It is therefore primarily an essay in interpretation for the benefit of students whose background is American or British. The task would be difficult enough even if Lukács had been less prolific as an author, but additional problems present themselves which must be frankly faced at the outset. Lukács is firmly within the Central European tradition of thought, a tradition whose assumptions for the most part have no precise equivalent in the English-speaking world. Moreover, while for the past half century committed to Marxism, he has substantially adhered to a Hegelian approach not generally accepted among Leninists, let alone Western Marxists, whatever their political affiliation.

Lukács' personal involvements after 1917, in his native Hungary and within the wider orbit of the Communist movement, have borne fruit in factional polemics which for him clearly had, and have, considerable significance, as may be inferred from the autobiographical notes and prefaces he has contributed in recent years to Western editions of his writings. In some instances he has taken the opportunity to withdraw or revise earlier judgments. In other cases he has made use of changes in the political climate for the purpose of repudiating, or describing as merely tactical, certain accommodations to the Stalinist orthodoxy prevalent in Eastern Europe during the 1930s and 1940s. An account of these tortuous maneuvers is to be found in the 1967 preface to volume II of his writings issued by a West German publishing house as part of an edition of his major works. This particular volume includes the essay collection entitled *Geschichte und Klassenbewusstsein* (*History and Class Consciousness*) whose appearance in 1923 brought Lukács into conflict with the nascent Soviet orthodoxy. While the 1967 preface repudiates his pre-Leninist philosophical standpoint, it also disinters various factional disputes of the same period, sets out a belated justification of certain political views he had put forward around 1928, and explicitly describes as merely tactical and non-serious the solemn autocritique he published a little later, when faced with the danger of being excluded from the Communist Party (a fate that subsequently overtook him in the wake of his brief participation in the ill-starred attempt to democratize the Hungarian regime in 1956).

In the interval Lukács had worked in the Moscow Marx-Engels Institute in 1930 and 1931, played an active part in the literary life of the German Communist Party in Berlin between 1931 and 1933, labored in the Philosophical Institute of the Moscow Academy of Sciences from 1933 to 1944, helped to edit literary publications, and thereafter returned to Hungary in the wake of the Soviet Army. While holding the chair of Aesthetics and Cultural Philosophy in Budapest under the regime of Mátyás Rákosi, he came under attack from ultra-Stalinists and gradually withdrew from active party life. With the post-Stalin "thaw" he emerged once again, and during the brief uprising of October–November 1956 became a member of the party's Central Committee and Education Minister in the government of Imre Nagy. Having survived the latter's fall and execution, he returned from a brief period of exile in Rumania and was allowed to resume a normal existence in Budapest under the government of János Kádár, although his writings fell under an official ban and had to be published in the West. Readmitted to the Communist Party in 1967, he was understood to have protested privately against the invasion and occupation of Czechoslovakia. In March 1969, on the fiftieth anniversary of the brief Hungarian Soviet Republic in 1919, in which he had participated, he was officially decorated with the Order of the Red Banner.

An attempt to take a synoptic view of Lukács' work since the opening years of the century discloses the fateful significance of the 1914–1918 war and the 1917 Russian revolution. It has become a platitude that these events terminated a way of life as well as a political balance of power. What needs some additional emphasis is the crucial position of Germany and Austria-Hungary. While Communism emerged from the turmoil of the Russian Revolution, and Fascism had forerunners in France and Italy before 1914, the decisive intellectual contribution was made by theorists domiciled in Germany and in the Dual Monarchy of Austria-Hungary plus its various successor states after 1918. In this perspective, Lukács may be said to have done for Communism what his contemporary Oswald Spengler did for the rival Fascist movement. After Lenin's death in 1924, Russian Communism produced few original thinkers, and none of global significance. In consequence, Lukács' intellectual heresies gradually assumed an importance they had not at first possessed. Central Europe being the principal arena of politico-ideological confrontation in the 1920s and 1930s, the passions stirred by these controversies gradually spread to wider circles. Within the domain of German socialism they were kept alive by the writings of Karl Korsch (who unlike Lukács eventually broke with the Communist International, although not with Marxism). They were likewise echoed in the historical and sociological studies published by the scholars associated with the Frankfurt Institut für Sozialforschung—notably Horkheimer, Adorno, and Marcuse.

The influence of the early Lukács is also discernible in the writings of Walter Benjamin, a noted literary critic of the Weimar period, and a more distant echo may be discerned in the work of *émigré* scholars such as Leo Lowenthal. From Central Europe, the message of Lukács' Hegelianized Marxism was carried to France by the Rumanian-born literary critic Lucien Goldmann, whose studies of Pascal and Racine acquainted the French academic world with a new manner of treating literary subjects. In contrast, Lukács has not in recent years exercised much influence upon the younger generation of Marxist writers in Central or Eastern Europe. In general they have found him too orthodox and in particular too deeply wedded to the notions current in Soviet literature. "Revisionist" writers (e.g., the veteran Austrian Communist Ernst Fischer) tend to go beyond

Lukács in trying to construct a specifically Marxist doctrine of the social relevance of art. In philosophy, too, it was the existentialism of Sartre rather than the work of Lukács which, after the post-Stalin "thaw" of 1956, enabled some among the younger East European Marxists (e.g., the Polish philosopher Leszek Kolakowski) to free themselves from the ideological trammels of Stalinism.

These circumstances are noted here not for the sake of whatever interest they may possess for the moralist, but to illustrate the difficulty of separating philosophy and politics in the work of George Lukács. A certain underlying consistency in his theoretical and practical commitments does emerge from the study of his voluminous writings. Equally, it appears possible to trace important elements of Lukács' thinking to his pre-1914 intellectual antecedents, his social background, and his spiritual inheritance as a member of the Hungarian Jewish intelligentsia. While these topics will be given a brief airing, I have on the whole attempted to center this study upon an analysis of the contribution Lukács has made to Marxist theory, notably in his chosen field of aesthetics. It is of course impossible to engage this theme in a spirit of scientific detachment, but while neutrality is excluded, one may aim at objectivity in the Hegelian sense: at an attempt, that is, to situate the uniquely determined significance of the phenomenon that goes under the name of George Lukács.

G.L.

London
November 1969

CONTENTS

The Heritage

●

i

György Lukács was born on April 13, 1885, of wealthy Jewish parents in Budapest, then the second capital of the Austro-Hungarian monarchy. His father was a director of the Budapest Kreditanstalt, at the time the leading bank in Hungary. A member of a remarkable generation of intellectuals, many of whom later emigrated and made their mark in the sciences and humanities, Lukács from adolescence displayed a lively interest in literature and a marked talent for criticism. His earliest writings date from 1902. He took an active share in the intellectual life of his native city while still in his early twenties, and a two-volume study on the modern drama, running to over a thousand pages, appeared in the Hungarian language in 1911. In the same year Lukács issued *Die Seele und die Formen* (*The Soul and the Forms*), the German-language edition of a philosophical study already published in Budapest a year earlier, and from this time he partly abandoned Hungarian in favor of German. In later years he came to be internationally known by the German form of his name, Georg Lukács, having originally signed his publications "von Lukács," with the title of nobility bestowed upon his father by the reigning dynasty.

A complex intellectual development carried Lukács from the aestheticism fashionable among Central European intellectuals before 1914 to a qualified acceptance of what was then known as *Lebensphilosophie*, a form of vitalism or intuitionism which stood at the opposite pole from scientific rationalism. As a student in Budapest (where he obtained a doctorate in philosophy in 1906) he had originally accepted the prevailing neo-Kantian doctrine which reserved the systematic investigation of empirical reality for the specialized arts and sciences, while restricting philosophy to logic and the theory of knowledge. However, by the time he attended lectures at Berlin University given by the philosopher and sociologist Georg Simmel (1909–1910), Lukács had begun to adopt the latter's highly personal interpretation of neo-Kantianism, itself rooted in the work of Wilhelm Windelband and Heinrich Rickert, whose lectures Lukács attended in Heidelberg in 1913 and 1914, when he likewise made the acquaintance of Rickert's and Windelband's most distinguished pupil, Emil Lask.

German intellectual life during those years before World War I centered upon the dissolution of the neo-Kantian school, the rise of phenomenology (Husserl), and the growth of irrationalist and intuitionist tendencies ultimately stemming from the Romantic movement. Kantian orthodoxy, as represented by Hermann Cohen and Paul Natorp at Marburg, stood for a rigid distinction between *Erkenntnistheorie* (theory of cognition) and speculative metaphysics. The Heidelberg school tended to allot more importance to history than to the natural sciences, and its influence facilitated the reception of what Wilhelm Dilthey (1833–1911) termed *Geisteswissenschaft*. The dispute turned upon the question whether philosophy might legitimately aim at something beyond the generalization of scientific method. Dilthey and Simmel represented a reaction against the positivism of the natural sciences, but also against the Marburg school, which denied the possibility of insight into the veritable nature of reality. Like their French contemporary Henri Bergson, whose *L'Évolution Créatrice* (1907) had a marked influence upon Simmel, they had come to believe that real essences were cognizable through an act of intellectual intuition.

What Dilthey's "science of spirit" stood for was something basically different from the rationalist methodology whereby the natural and social sciences "explained" the world in causal terms. As he saw it, the historian's task lay in a "hermeneutic" understanding of the past through an act of imaginative recovery of other men's thoughts. To understand was to transfer oneself to a different spiritual dimension, an operation which Dilthey— following the romantic theology of Schleiermacher— termed reliving (*Nacherleben*). This ultimately personal and irrational act of spiritual reconstruction was conceived as a method proper to the humanities. Hermeneutics signified a mode of understanding not dependent upon causal explanation. Rather it aimed at the interpretation of multiform creations of the human spirit. Works of the mind possessed a hidden significance which *Geisteswissenschaft* must set itself to decipher. Dilthey's approach had at first originated in psychology, a circumstance which induced Windelband in 1894 to utter a warning against confusing the naturalistic search for general laws with the truly historical analysis of the singular and unique event. His later writings reflected the impact of Edmund Husserl's radical rejection of psychologism. What he termed *Geisteswissenschaft* had from the start been conceived as a philosophic enterprise. In this fashion Dilthey eventually arrived at the category of signification (*Bedeutung*) which enabled him to postulate an objective relation between particular data (e.g., works of art) and the history of the human spirit.

For all its originality, Dilthey's enterprise was solidly rooted in a specifically German tradition: that of the historical school which in the earlier nineteenth century had been associated with the names of Humboldt, Niebuhr, Savigny, Grimm, and Schleiermacher. What the school affirmed was the autonomy of history, anthropology, and the study of religion, as against the positivist search for causal laws applicable to nature and history alike. This approach had an important corollary: all individual manifestations were seen as belonging to an ordered or structural whole, whereas the positivism of the natural sciences tended to regard them as exemplifications of a general rule. For obvious reasons, the historical approach—like the Romantic philosophy in general—was more satisfying to artists than to scientists, and the revolt against rationalism typically made use of concepts derived from the model of artistic creation. At the same time the "holistic" emphasis on the dependence of the parts upon the totality had implications for the social sciences. Windelband, Rickert, Dilthey, and Simmel gradually elaborated a distinction between "nature" and "culture" which explicitly renounced the search for "laws of development." Their writings in turn fortified Max Weber (1864–1920) in his search for a sociological method which would take account of the meaning that individual actions possess for others. Weber's description of sociology as an attempt to understand social activities "on the level of meaning" (*deutend verstehen*) was clearly related to the work of the scholars already mentioned.

In his early writings Lukács made his bow to this methodology, having already in his literary essays discussed the poetry of the Romantics. In later years he was to deplore this phase as a youthful aberration and to characterize his early philosophy as "subjective idealism," a term commonly reserved for doctrines derived from Kant. His autobiographical reflections on this topic must, however, be treated with a certain reserve, for there is some evidence that after his student years he was never genuinely a neo-Kantian: that is to say, an agnostic for whom the universe was in the last resort not wholly cognizable. The author of *The Soul and the Forms* appears to have believed that in the aesthetic sphere, at least, one might attain contact with ultimate reality through an act of immediate intuition. "Far from being the subjective idealist of his later 'self-criticism,' he was evidently most influenced by the semi-phenomenological position of Emil Lask at Heidelberg, an influence that later facilitated his shift to the objective idealism of Hegel."[1]

This refers to the period in 1913 and 1914 when Lukács had settled in Heidelberg and become a member of the circle around Max Weber. Emil Lask (1875–1915) was then professor of philosophy in Heidelberg, and Lukács inevitably came under his spell. Lask's major work, *Die Logik der Philosophie und die Kategorien-*

[1] Morris Watnick, "Relativism and Class Consciousness: Georg Lukács," p. 142.

lehre (1910), furnished a logical foundation for a species of neo-Platonism to which Lukács had already become an instinctive convert. This in turn opened the path to a logically defensible belief in a supersensible realm of being. Lask's studies in ethics, aesthetics, and the philosophy of religion—interrupted in 1914 by the war in which he met his death a year later—had brought him into the vicinity of Edmund Husserl's phenomenological school. Lukács' intellectual development during these years was profoundly marked by Lask, his senior in years and a thinker of uncommon power and penetration, who had gradually shifted to a viewpoint that could properly be described as metaphysical.

Tendencies in this direction were not unusual around 1910, but it was the war of 1914–1918 that brought matters to a head. In the agony of these years a professorial philosophy which compartmentalized knowledge inevitably lost whatever authority it had once possessed. There were indeed men such as Weber who affirmed that a return to metaphysics was impossible, but the young generation demanded a "total" system of truth about the world. Among writers with philosophical inclinations this quest led some to religion, others to Nietzsche's irrationalism, still others to a nihilistic rejection of culture as a whole. Lukács, for reasons that will shortly become apparent, moved in a different direction: toward Hegel. It is noteworthy that his philosophical work originated in literary criticism. He had during these years become a member of the esoteric circle around the poet Stefan George, and nothing was further from the minds of these men than the thought of political involvement. Disciples of Goethe, Nietzsche, and *fin de siècle* poets with mystical leanings, they cultivated an individualism that found its legitimation in a profound distaste for the world of ordinary men. A similar attitude underlay Lukács' major literary production during this period, his *Theory of the Novel*.[2]

The mood in which the youthful Lukács composed this work in 1914 and 1915, while still at Heidelberg and remote from political activity, may be inferred from the preface contributed to a currently available West German reprint. Dated "Budapest, July 1962," this foreword, for all its dutiful self-criticism, does not entirely repudiate the spirit in which Lukács had in those days sought refuge from actuality in the realm of art. For what hope was there in the political world? If the three Eastern Empires (Russia, Austria-Hungary, and Germany) went down in consequence of the war, well and good. "But then the question arises: who is going to save us from Western civilization?" In thus retrospectively describing his attitude during the opening phase of World War I, Lukács supplied readers with the key to his lifelong admiration for Thomas Mann, with the obvious qualification that Mann in those days did not simply fear the West's triumph over the German *Reich:* he wanted Germany to win (see his *Unpolitical Reflections* of 1918)! Lukács detested bourgeois liberalism and what he regarded as Western decadence no less than Thomas Mann did in those years, but unlike Mann he had no use for Wilhelminian Germany. Hence his critical study of 1914–15 reflected what in 1962 he termed "a mood of permanent despair about the condition of the world. It was only in 1917 that I obtained an an-

---

[2] *Die Theorie des Roman: Ein geschichtsphilosophischer Versuch über die Formen der grossen Epik.* Originally drafted in 1914 and 1915, the work made its first appearance in 1916 in Max Dessoir's *Zeitschrift für Ästhetik und Allgemeine Kunstwissenschaft* and appeared in book form in 1920. For an extract from it dealing with the problem of form in epic and dramatic art see *Georg Lukács—Schriften zur Literatursoziologie,* pp. 89 ff.

swer to questions which until then had appeared insoluble." The Russian Revolution resolved his metaphysical anguish by giving a practical answer to theoretical problems which had induced him to withdraw into a private shell. *The Theory of the Novel* had been a product of the mental outlook associated with what was then known among Dilthey's followers as *Geistesgeschichte* (history of the spirit). The war brought matters to a head, but the problematic already existed. As Lukács put it in 1962:

> Today it is no longer difficult to perceive clearly the limitations of the hermeneutic method. One can indeed also comprehend its relative historical justification as against the pettiness and shallowness of neo-Kantian or other positivism, whether in its treatment of historical figures or contexts, or of intellectual structures (logic, aesthetics, etc.). I am thinking, for example, of the fascination exerted by Dilthey's *Das Erlebnis und die Dichtung* (Leipzig, 1905), a work which in many respects appeared to break new ground. This new realm appeared to us in those days as a mental universe of grandiose syntheses, theoretically as well as historically. We failed to perceive how far this new method was from having overcome positivism, how insecurely its syntheses were based. . . . It became the fashion to construct general synthetic concepts from what in most cases was a mere intuitive perception of a few tendencies peculiar to some movement or period.

And yet his early work had not been worthless. Writing in 1962 Lukács could perceive at least one hopeful feature: the youthful author was even then on his way to his later standpoint:

> It has already been noted that the author . . . had become a Hegelian. The older leading representatives

of the hermeneutic method stood on a Kantian foundation and were not free from positivist residues;
Dilthey above all. And the attempt to overcome the
shallowness of positivist rationalism nearly always
signified a step towards irrationalism; notably in
Simmel's case, but also with Dilthey. It is true that
the Hegel renaissance had already begun a few years
before the war . . . but . . . principally in the field of
logic or the general theory of science. So far as I am
aware, the *Theorie des Romans* is the first work in the
domain of spiritual interpretation in which Hegelian
philosophy was concretely applied to aesthetic problems.

Professor Victor Zitta, in his relentlessly hostile study,
suggests that Lukács, having failed to become either a
poet (in Hungary before 1910) or a philosopher (in
Germany around 1914), settled for being an essayist
and literary critic "active in a domain of intellectual
life where excellence does not necessarily bring fame
and where creativity and significance do not come the
easy way, where genius is muffled by the fact that it
has to subordinate itself to commentary and analysis."[3]
Without going quite so far, it does seem noteworthy that
Lukács' early work, for all its undeniable brilliance, fails
to exhibit the kind of sustained logical power to be found
in Lask. *The Soul and the Forms* had been a remarkable
tour de force for a young man of twenty-five, and it had
earned its author a reputation among Hungary's intellectual elite, even though it may be the case that poetry
was valued more highly by Hungarians than Platonizing
essays on art. Quite possibly Lukács, who helped to
organize the Thalia theater in Budapest while still a
teen-ager, would have liked to become a poet or a drama-
tist, until he reluctantly settled for the role of critic. As

[3] Victor Zitta, *Georg Lukács' Marxism*; pp. 24–25.

such he attained distinction before he had worked out a philosophical approach of his own. *The Theory of the Novel* impressed discerning readers—this time in Germany—and won its author the lasting esteem of Germany's greatest novelist, Thomas Mann. But as Lukács himself recognized in later years, it was a young man's work: basically derivative and dependent on notions acquired at second hand. When we come to Lukács' most controversial work, the 1923 essay collection entitled *History and Class Consciousness*, we shall see that its strictly philosophical content was mediated by Lask's interpretation of Kant, Fichte, and Hegel; its politics and economics were taken over bodily from Lenin and Rosa Luxemburg (the incompatibility of these two great Marxists was not yet plain to him); and its criticism of Engels' "dialectical materialism" was subsequently abandoned in response to pressing demands for intellectual conformity. Nor can one overlook the circumstance that it was Dilthey who had originally opened Lukács' eyes to the radical difference between natural science and history: the uniqueness of the historical event and the need to apprehend it in all its concreteness by an act of reliving which might be said to have an intellectual as well as an aesthetic dimension. In noting all this one simply registers the fact that while Lukács distinguished himself at an early age by productions of considerable brilliance, one cannot say that he manifested the kind of originality which commonly marks even the immature productions of genius. *The Theory of the Novel* is no exception. It is an exquisitely talented piece of writing, and that is all.

From Hermeneutics to Politics

● ●

11

A critical study devoted to an important writer frequently begins with a brief biographical sketch and thereafter concentrates upon an analysis of his work. Anyone who tries to apply this procedure to Lukács is bound to discover that the method breaks down. The private existence of even the most cloistered scholar cannot be wholly dissociated from his public standing, and when the writer in question has spent half a century in the service of a revolutionary cause, it is plain that the distinction between "life" and "thought" becomes untenable. If in addition his most important work as a theorist concerns problems stemming from the convulsions of European history since 1914, how is one to separate theory from practice? The decade from 1914 to 1924 witnessed the greatest upheaval Europe had undergone since Napoleon; no excuse is needed for adopting the historical approach in considering Lukács' work during this eventful period. Even so there has to be some rather drastic simplification. We shall try to analyze the transformation of the youthful neo-Platonist of 1914 into the Marxist theoretician of 1924, while leaving until later his strictly political and organizational involvements.

One of the difficulties a study of Lukács has to face is the discrepancy between his standing as a theorist in Continental Europe and the predominant view taken of his significance in the English-speaking world. This is not a political issue, and it involves no judgment on the respective merits of his earlier and later writings. There exists a fairly widespread notion in the West—entertained both by his more thoughtless admirers and by some of his critics—that Lukács has throughout his career been primarily a theorist of aesthetics who for accidental personal reasons threw in his lot with the Communist Party. This curious misconception has its roots in a failure to take seriously the kind of theorizing which traditionally has provided the intellectual groundwork of Continental European thinking. That literature and the arts are significant only insofar as they body forth eternal truths and absolute values is indeed a conviction common to political and theological conservatives in many lands. But this kind of conservatism has for long been on the defensive. Its enemies have included relativist philosophers as well as impressionistic writers unwilling to grant aesthetics the status of a genuine theory anchored in the perception of verities independent of the critic's personal standpoint. What is currently known as empiricism commonly goes with liberalism in politics and subjectivism in morals: art is its own justification, and aesthetics is simply the descriptive analysis of what constitutes the autonomy of art.

Now it needs to be said that—irrespective of political attitudes distributed over the entire ideological spectrum from Communism to Fascism—the Anglo-American world has for long appeared to Continental Europeans as a "de-centered totality," to employ the currently fashionable jargon. It is to them a philistine culture with a void at the center, lacking anything worth being called a philosophy, i.e., any kind of conceptual thinking that tries to make sense of life as a whole, or even of the social order in which culture is embedded. What passes for philosophy in the English-speaking world appears from this standpoint as at best an interesting exercise in logical analysis, and at worst as an academic parlor game. American and British empiricists in turn commonly react to this kind of criticism by dismissing metaphysics as antiquated nonsense, Hegelian philosophy as a fraud, and Marxism as its illegitimate offspring.

One consequence of this mutual incomprehension is that anyone who sets out to interpret the work of George Lukács for the English-speaking public must at some point affirm what outside the Anglo-American world is regarded as a truism: namely that science cannot take the place traditionally occupied by the great metaphysical systems. If these systems are dead, there is no hope of replacing them by logical or linguistic analysis. But a further consequence also follows, namely that the void cannot be filled by the study of literature. That this desperate attempt should actually have been made during the past half century testifies to the fact that even in a culture estranged from its own past men do not live by the worship of facts alone. But for all the very great progress that has been made in elevating literary criticism to the status of genuine theorizing there clearly is no hope of making it do the work of conceptual "totalization" in the Hegelian-Marxian sense (or for that matter in the Kierkegaardian or Barthian sense). Literature and art cannot take the place of philosophy and religion, although they may transmit the values of both or either. It was precisely this discovery that drove the youthful Lukács out of his ivory tower, albeit the direction he took was fortuitous in the sense of being determined by the politics of his native Hungary, and by the key role of an intelligentsia which for obvious reasons could not opt for the romantic irrationalism of the political Right.

In reserving politics for separate treatment, we follow the logic of Lukács' own development, for it was only in 1924 that he became a full-fledged Leninist. Until then he sought to combine an "ultra-left" political standpoint (to adopt Communist parlance) with a rather personal interpretation of Marxism, impressively formulated in the heretical essay collection of 1923. A brief sketch of the founder of Bolshevism, occasioned by Lenin's death in January 1924, signalized a tactical retreat from an untenable position, thereby enabling Lukács to preserve his official standing within the international Communist movement. But for the moment we are concerned with Lukács' intellectual development during the 1914–1924 period, and if this artificial dissection obliges us to discuss his politics after 1919 separately, the fault must in part be imputed to Lukács. Having come to Marx via Hegel, and then to Lenin by way of renouncing the highly original doctrine he had set out earlier in *History and Class Consciousness*, Lukács had to all appearances transformed himself so thoroughly by 1924 as to have shed his ancient self. In actual fact the political conversion to Leninism did not obliterate his pre-1914 commitment to the truth of certain general propositions about the nature of the world and the destiny of man. These truths to Lukács were absolute, objective, and nonempirical. Their validity was guaranteed neither by "science" in the positivist sense of the term nor by blind irrational faith, but by insight into the veritable nature of reality: an intellectual operation of which Hegel's philosophy furnished the model.

To the average adherent of what passes for common-sensible thinking in the English-speaking world, this kind of talk inevitably sounds rather too grandiose. It is therefore all the more important to emphasize that from the standpoint of most Central European thinkers of the period—for the Nietzscheans as well as the Hegelians, for Spengler and Heidegger no less than Lukács—common-sensible reasoning of the empiricist variety was the enemy. There was of course a massive core of positivist thinking in the natural sciences which had barely been affected by the crisis in the humanities; there were influential figures—Max Weber being the best known—who consistently adhered to the rigorous neo-Kantian divorce between scientific reasoning and metaphysics; there were likewise prominent neo-Kantians or positivists among the Social Democrats in Germany and Austria, where their party held a key position in politics during the 1920s. But these intellectual positions had already been undermined before 1914, and after 1918 they were exposed to increasingly violent assaults from all points of the political compass. In casting his lot with the revolutionary cause, Lukács made a political commitment that was in tune with philosophical convictions toward which he had been groping years before the Russian Revolution altered the European landscape.

Lukács had originally arrived on the scene at a time when it was generally held that the only choice open to one who could accept neither traditional metaphysics nor religious faith lay between the positivism of empirical science and the vitalism (there is no precise equivalent of *Lebensphilosophie*) of irrationalists such as

Nietzsche or Bergson. Dissatisfaction with this sort of alternative was fairly widespread in the academic milieu, whence the fascination of what Dilthey had accomplished in the domain of *Geisteswissenschaft*: an untranslatable term, since *Geist* carries metaphysical overtones very inadequately rendered by "mind" or "spirit." What *Geisteswissenschaft* ultimately implied was the identity of the reflective thinker's own mind with the Mind whose manifestations lie spread out before us in history. In this sense, hermeneutics of the type represented by Dilthey could be seen as an attempt to restore to philosophy the central position it had possessed in Hegel's time (minus Hegel's spiritualist ontology, which Dilthey, in this respect faithful to his neo-Kantian heritage, rejected as arbitrary and speculative).

What distinguished *Geisteswissenschaft* from *Naturwissenschaft* was its method no less than its theme. If the natural sciences operated with a clear-cut distinction between subject and object, mind and matter, a "science of spirit" was necessarily reflective and introspective, its topic being the world created by the (human) spirit. The distinction went back to Giambattista Vico, as did the related notion that there is—or at any rate there can be—a science of mind which is at once the mirror of the soul and the record of man's development. Hegel had fused these metaphysical assumptions into a grandiose system which lost its authority during the later nineteenth century, having come under fire from positivist historians, sociologists, and anthropologists. When the neo-Kantian revival of the 1870s reinstated philosophy, it did so on the understanding that the philosopher would henceforth not lay claim to insights hidden from the scientist. Philosophy, then, was virtually synonymous with the logic of science: a position common to the

neo-Kantians and to positivist Marxists such as Engels.[1]
It was a mounting concern over this radical disjunction
between science and *Weltanschauung*—that is to say,
philosophy in the grand manner—which after 1900
brought about a renewed interest in Hegel, to which
Dilthey contributed powerfully with a deeply penetrating
biographical and critical study of Hegel's early writings.[2]
In so doing he effected a final rupture with his own
positivist beginnings and at the same time crowned an
impressive body of work which may be said to have revolved around a single central theme: the reconstitution
of that union of theory and practice, logic and ethic, the
empirical and the transcendental, which Kant had torn
asunder. The study of history disclosed the essential
nature of man as it unfolded in the totality of human
experience, and the historian entered into the life of
past generations by reliving in his own mind the
thoughts and actions whereby men had once defined
themselves. *Geisteswissenschaft* and *Lebensphilosophie*,

[1] See Engels' publications of the 1870s and 1880s, notably
the *Anti-Düring* (1878) and his tract on Feuerbach (1888).
The statement, however, does not hold for Engels' posthu-
mously published writings on the dialectics of nature (*Dialektik der Natur*, 1873–1882), which among other things
represented an attempt to salvage the heritage of the romantic "philosophy of nature" developed earlier in the century by some contemporaries of Hegel and Schelling. There
was an unresolved conflict in the mind of Engels, who in
this respect was fairly representative of many educated
Germans of his time.
[2] Dilthey, *Die Jugendgeschichte Hegels* (1906). A comparison
of this study with Lukács' work *Der junge Hegel* (1948)
illuminates not only the mental process Lukács underwent
after parting company with Dilthey, but also the decline in
scholarly standards during the Stalinist era, when Lukács'
book was composed. Originally completed in manuscript by
1938, it saw the light a decade later, by which time Lukács
was back in Budapest but had not yet come under fire as a
"revisionist."

"science of spirit" and "philosophy of life," were two aspects of one untiring search for a supra-empirical vision of the living and moving totality of world history.

What the neo-Kantian separation of "theoretical and practical Reason" had signified for the youthful Lukács (and not for him alone) may be inferred from the opening passage of *The Theory of the Novel*:

> Blessed are the times when the firmament is a road map whose contours mark the way to be followed and whose paths are illuminated by the stars. . . . The world is wide and yet resembles one's own abode, for the fire burning in the soul is consubstantial with the stars. . . . "Philosophy is really nostalgia," says Novalis, "the desire to be at home everywhere." Hence philosophy as a form of existence [*Lebensform*] . . . is always symptomatic of a rift between the interior and the exterior, a sign of the essential difference [*Wesensverschiedenheit*] of the ego and the world, the incongruity of the soul and the deed.

The lyrical note, appropriate to a youthful author brought up on the Romantics and the *fin-de-siècle* Symbolists, both revealed and concealed an authentic spiritual dilemma. Unlike Dilthey, who had been raised in a Calvinist milieu and studied Protestant theology before turning to philosophy, Lukács possessed neither a religious background nor an instinctive affinity with the side of nineteenth-century German idealist metaphysics which may fairly be described as secularized faith. His existential despair could find expression only in the dimension of a lyricism nurtured on Hölderlin, Hegel's unfortunate poet-friend whose life terminated in madness. The truths Lukács sought down to 1917 were by their nature unsuited to a more prosaic form of expression. His subsequent adoption of a resolutely didactic manner modeled on Hegel was meant to veil the continuity, but later critics have not failed to perceive the link between the youthful and the mature Lukács, in the all-important (to him) domain of aesthetics.[3] A reviewer of *The Soul and the Forms* had already made the point in 1912 that Lukács was essentially a Symbolist. "Beginning with questions of poetic technique, Lukács aims at a philosophy of art in order thus to pinpoint the ultimate questions of life."[4]

This approach was common enough in the circles in which he then moved. In all essentials it had for long been promoted by the more self-conscious of Goethe's spiritual descendants, notably the greatest of them: Thomas Mann. What needs to be stressed is that Lukács in these years moved toward Hegelianism for reasons similar to those that had induced Dilthey to abandon the neo-Kantianism dominant in the German academic world before the war. The vital difference lay in the fact that Dilthey had been profoundly rooted in the German Protestant middle-class culture of the later nineteenth century, whereas Lukács felt spiritually adrift in an age when bourgeois civilization—the only civilization he ever understood or appreciated—was disintegrating. In casting himself as Dilthey's Marxist successor—not that he ever made an explicit claim to this effect, but this was in fact what he was doing—Lukács fell heir to the unsolved problems of *Geisteswissenschaft* and *Lebensphilosophie* alike: how could metaphysical certitudes be extracted from the study of history if historical investigation issued in the recognition that every culture had

[3] Victor Zitta, *Georg Lukács' Marxism*, pp. 37 ff.; Peter Demetz, *Marx, Engels und die Dichter* (Stuttgart, 1959), chap. VIII. See also Demetz, "Zwischen Klassik und Bolschewismus," *Merkur*, June 1958; George Steiner, "Georg Lukács and his Devil's Pact," *Kenyon Review*, Winter 1960.
[4] "Georg Lukács: Die Seele und die Formen," *Logos*, III (1912), 249.

its own norms which entered into the perception of reality? For Dilthey the answer resolved itself in an act of faith: not in the theological beliefs of his youth, but in the quasi-mystical monism of Herder, Goethe, Schelling, Schleiermacher, and Humboldt. *Geisteswissenschaft* centered in an act of *Verstehen* (understanding) of *Erlebnis* in which the individual thinker transcended the psychological level and reconstituted the objective meaning of the spirit-world, as it manifested itself in the various national cultures with their distinctive arts, sciences, philosophies, and religions. These objectivations of spirit, which in their totality made up the human world, were constantly in motion, but nonetheless represented a suprahistorical realm accessible to the reflective mind; and they could be understood for the simple reason that the contemplative thinker was himself an actor in the process whereby the universal mind differentiated itself into a multitude of individual minds.[5]

It was in this sense that Lukács in 1962 described his *Theory of the Novel* as "a typical representative of *Geisteswissenschaft*." Dilthey's hermeneutic method had then been his own. The method, briefly explicated by Dilthey in an essay of 1900, represented an attempt to replace the psychological approach by a systematic interpretation (*hermeneia*) of the symbolic structures the historian encounters in confronting the creations of mind or spirit. But where Dilthey had contented himself with a typology of world-views ultimately rooted in unchanging psychic structures, Lukács went all the way back to

[5] Dilthey, "Die Enstehung der Hermeutik," in *Gesammelte Schriften*, vol. V. Jürgen Habermas, in *Erkenntnis und Interesse* (Frankfurt, 1968), pp. 178 ff., notes that Dilthey's later work was indebted to Edmund Husserl's *Logische Untersuchungen*, which when they first appeared in 1900 initiated a salutary reaction against the attempt to dissolve logical categories into psychology, in the empiricist manner.

Hegel. Dilthey had specified three basic types of *Weltanschauung*: an aesthetic-contemplative one (also described as "objective idealism"); an activist one, exemplified by the "subjective idealism" of Fichte; and a naturalist realism, represented in his own age by the positivism of Comte and Spencer. These distinctions were Kantian rather than Hegelian, in that they were meant to portray permanent characters of the human mind. In going beyond them, Lukács revived the Hegelian idea of a self-activating process inherent in the dialectical motion of spirit. The 1962 preface to *The Theory of the Novel* is explicit on this point:

> There is of course also a positivist, a historical relativism, and it was precisely during the war years that Spengler fused it with *geisteswissenschaftliche* tendencies, so as to arrive at a radical historization of all the categories, refusing to recognize any supra-historical validity, whether aesthetic, ethical or logical. . . . The author of the *Theorie des Romans* does not go as far as that. He was searching for an historically based universal dialectic of the genres—rooted in the essence of the aesthetic categories, in the essence of the literary forms—that would tend towards a more intimate interrelation of the categories and history than he had encountered in Hegel; he was trying to conceive something stable within the flux (*ein Beharren im Wechsel*), an internal transformation within the permanency of essence (*eine innere Verwandlung innerhalb des Geltendbleibens des Wesens*).

In thus describing his intellectual beginnings, Lukács might arguably have made the further point that his proto-Hegelianism had been anticipated by Dilthey, insofar as it rested on Vico's dictum that men are able to understand only that which they have made: *verum et factum convertuntur*. Dilthey had explicitly invoked Vico against Descartes and the Cartesian method generally, and in so doing revived a methodological principle common to Hegel and Marx (with the important difference that for Hegel, as for Vico and the scholastics before him, the philosophy of history assumed a retrospective function: the mind recognizes the inner logic of the historical process only after the event).[6] For Vico, in this respect still rooted in the cult of antiquity, the logic of history manifested itself in the cyclical motion of *corso* and *ricorso*. For the French eighteenth-century heirs of Cartesianism, headed by Turgot and Condorcet, history signified a unilinear progress toward a this-worldly state of perfection. Hegel had synthesized Vico's approach with the creed of the Enlightenment, but while he abandoned the belief in a cyclical motion, he retained the conviction that Spirit comes to self-consciousness in philosophy only after an epoch has reached its term: Minerva's owl flies out at dusk, as he put it in the preface to his *Philosophy of Right*; or, to cite Marx's rather less flattering characterization of Hegel's procedure, "The philosopher comes *post festum*." What distinguished the Young Hegelians of the 1840s from Hegel was the conviction that history could be *made*: not blindly, as in the past—for of course men had in a certain sense always "made" their own history, though they had not been aware of it—but with full consciousness. Marx was not the only radical of his time who broke with Hegel on this issue, but the rupture he effected assumed world-historical significance because it meshed with the theory and practice of a movement that aimed to transform the world. In recovering this dimension of Marx's

[6] See Habermas, *op. cit.*, p. 188; and the same author's *Theorie und Praxis*, pp. 206 ff.

thought, which had been diluted by his followers and was barely recognizable in the evolutionist outlook of European socialism in 1914, Lukács followed the logic of an argument already set out in the 1845 *Theses on Feuerbach.*

Why then did it take World War I, and more specifically the Russian Revolution, to break the spell of contemplative *Geisteswissenschaft*? The 1962 preface to *The Theory of the Novel* makes the interesting point that Lukács in those years was "essentially influenced by Sorel." Now Georges Sorel (1847–1922) had come to the attention of the wider public with his *Réflexions sur la violence* (1906–1908), whose animadversions upon the shallowness of bourgeois liberalism fitted in with the then fashionable disparagement of material progress. Here we touch upon the peculiar ambiguity of the German term *Geist*. When taken in the sense of "spirit," *Geist* is not simply different from material reality, but superior to it. In pre-1914 Germany it was well understood among intellectuals with conservative and romantic leanings that German *Kultur* differed from West European *civilization* in that it gave primacy to *Geist*. But *Geist* was contemplative rather than active. As Dilthey used the term, *Geistesgeschichte* might indeed portray the "spirit of the age" as it manifested itself in all the arts and sciences, but the historian could not transform the reality of his own age. Intellectual history (a possible translation of *Geistesgeschichte*, though not the only one) can and does reconstruct the various objectivations of spirit, from religion to changing fashions in art, but it is powerless to alter the material circumstances which have given birth to a particular culture and its prevailing "spirit."

On Dilthey's suppositions concerning the course of

events since the Renaissance liberated the human mind from theological blinkers, this disjunction between history and historiography presented no particular problem. He was enough of a nineteenth-century liberal to hold that progress was real. Mankind was gradually becoming conscious of its essential unity, and its self-awareness found expression in the perception of the ongoing process known as history. "The historical consciousness breaks the last chains, the chains which philosophy and natural science could never break. Now man is wholly free." *Geistesgeschichte*, the universal history of the human spirit, furnished proof that mankind had come of age. The relativism lurking just below the surface of this sort of consciousness became a problem for Germans only after Dilthey had left the scene. His typology of world-views satisfied his private craving for certitude. "We are able to know what the human spirit is only through history . . . this historical self-consciousness allows us to formulate a systematic theory of man." On this placid assumption the contemplative mode of thought was not merely proper to the historian: it likewise contented the philosopher. Historicism furnished its own justification by laying bare the innate structures of the human psyche. These structures mirrored themselves in the history of philosophy, where the same basic modes of thought were eternally in conflict. This approach rejoined Hegel's insight, but the Hegelian principle of becoming was lacking. On the other hand, Dilthey shared Hegel's quietism. He had perceived the logic of the process and that was enough for him.

On Hegel's Platonizing assumptions, the circular motion of Spirit, which first creates the world and then comes to self-awareness in philosophy, permits only one mode of thought: the contemplative one. Consider the way he puts it, with unsurpassed force and conviction, in the concluding passage of the *Phenomenology of Mind* (1807):

> The goal, which is Absolute Knowledge or Spirit knowing itself as Spirit, finds its pathway in the recollection of spiritual forms [*Geister*] as they are in themselves and as they accomplish the organization of their spiritual kingdom. Their conservation, looked at from the side of their free existence appearing in the form of contingency, is *History*; looked at from the side of their intellectually comprehended organization, it is the *Science* of the ways in which knowledge appears. Both together, or History [intellectually] comprehended [*begriffen*], form at once the recollection and the Golgotha of Absolute Spirit, the reality, the truth, the certainty of its throne, without which it were lifeless, solitary and alone. Only
>
> > The chalice of this realm of spirits
> > Foams forth to God his own Infinitude.

The verse is an adaptation of Schiller's celebrated lines (*"Aus dem Kelch des ganzen Seelenreiches schäumt ihm die Unendlichkeit"*) which historians of philosophy have treated as a romantic rendering of the theme of Plato's *Timaeus*. While Hegel took some liberties with Schiller's text (his own version runs *"Aus dem Kelche dieses Geisterreiches schäumt ihm seine Unendlichkeit"*), he conserved the spirit of the poet's utterance. A God who creates a world of finite spirits is a God who is not sufficient unto himself. The secret of German idealism lay in the conviction that the essence of this God could be understood by the human spirit. This esoteric faith served its purpose during the nineteenth century, but while its Platonizing message appealed to artists, it necessarily failed to make contact with the critical impulse engendered by the collapse of contemplative aestheticism in 1914:

> This is why in the *Theory of the Novel* the present era is not characterized in Hegelian terms, but—to employ Fichte's formulation—as "an age of utter degradation." But this ethically coloured pessimism about history did not signify a general retreat from Hegel to Fichte, but rather an infusion of Kierkegaard's thought into Hegel's dialectic of history. For the author of *The Theory of the Novel* Kierkegaard possessed considerable significance. . . . During the years spent in Heidelberg on the eve of the war, he worked on a study of Kierkegaard's critique of Hegel, which however was never completed. If these facts are mentioned here, it is not for biographical reasons, but in order to pinpoint a tendency which later assumed importance in German thought. The direct influence of Kierkegaard, it is true, led to the existentialism of Heidegger and Jaspers, hence to a more or less overt antagonism towards Hegel. But one ought not to forget that the Hegel renaissance was itself energetically at work in trying to represent Hegel as having been close to irrationalism. This tendency is already noticeable in Dilthey's studies on the young Hegel [Lukács, 1962].

This self-characterization differs markedly from the autobiographical essay "Mein Weg zu Marx" which Lukács contributed in 1933 to the Communist periodical *Internationale Literatur*. There the reader learned that the youthful Lukács, having read the *Communist Manifesto* while still a pupil at the Gymnasium, was sufficiently impressed to tackle not only Marx's political pamphlets but also the first volume of *Capital*, and was deeply impressed by the doctrine of surplus value and the theory of class conflict. At the same time, his conversion to socialism had no effect upon his basic outlook, for reasons which Lukács in 1933 described as follows:

> As is only natural in the case of a bourgeois intellectual, this influence was restricted to economics and especially "sociology." Materialist philosophy—I did not then draw any distinction between dialectical and undialectical materialism—I regarded as wholly antiquated in respect of the theory of cognition. The neo-Kantian doctrine of the 'immanence of consciousness' corresponded very well to my then class position and world view. I did not subject it to any sort of critical examination and accepted it unquestioningly as the starting-point of any kind of epistemological inquiry. I did indeed have reservations concerning extreme subjective idealism (the Marburg school of neo-Kantianism as well as Mach's philosophy), since I did not see how the question of reality could simply be treated as an immanent category of consciousness. But this did not lead to materialist conclusions, but rather towards those philosophical schools which tried to solve this problem in an irrationalist-relativist fashion, occasionally tending towards mysticism (Windelband-Rickert, Simmel, Dilthey). The influence of Simmel, whose pupil I then was, enabled me to integrate those elements of Marx's thought which I had assimilated during this period into such a *Weltanschauung*.[7]

In thus explaining that his indifference to materialist philosophy was only natural to a youthful bourgeois intellectual of the pre-1914 era, Lukács must have puzzled those among his readers who remembered that in 1923 (four years after he had played a leading role in the abortive Hungarian revolution of 1919) he was still not disposed to take "dialectical materialism" seriously. Some of them may also have wondered why it should

[7] *Georg Lukács—Schriften zur Ideologie und Politik*, pp. 323–24.

have been so easy for a youthful offspring of the *haute bourgeoisie* before 1914 to accept the Marxian doctrine of class conflict while resisting the comparatively harmless tenets of philosophical materialism. But one must remember that in 1933 Lukács was addressing a captive audience, and moreover felt bound to repudiate his youthful idealism, while affirming that even then he was not unaware of Marx. "Simmel's *Philosophy of Money* and Max Weber's writings on Protestantism supplied the model for a 'sociology of literature' wherein the necessarily diluted and pallid elements taken over from Marx were still present, albeit barely perceptible." Indeed the Marxian elements are so imperceptible that not even Lukács' staunchest followers have been able to identify them. The truth is that during those years before World War I Lukács was torn between the neo-Kantianism of Lask, the neo-Hegelianism of Dilthey, the religious irrationalism of Kierkegaard, and the aestheticism of the circle around Gundolf and George; while his political thinking reflected the influence of Sorel, who was then philosophically an admirer of Bergson. None of this is discreditable, but one cannot explain it in terms relevant to his "class position." It would be truer to say that his spiritual anguish was the mirror of a civilization then about to undergo its first great crisis.

War and Revolution

III

From what has been said in the foregoing chapter some readers may be tempted to infer that the author of *History and Class Consciousness* was a prominent Marxist theorist and only incidentally a Hungarian who acquired his basic philosophical training in pre-1914 Germany. This impression must be corrected by going back to the earliest sources of Lukács' political and philosophical evolution. We have noted before that this procedure involves an artificial distinction between closely related topics: Lukács' gradual retreat from aestheticism after 1914, and his political involvements during the decade 1919–29. The crucial date is 1919, when he was prominent in the brief Hungarian Soviet Republic as Deputy Commissar of Culture and—more important—as a leading figure in the newly founded Communist Party. In his official capacity he briefly occupied a notable part of the political foreground, but the decisive plunge into party affairs occurred off-stage and has been accorded less attention. Moreover, it is only in recent years that light has fallen on the crucial share taken in Lukács' intellectual development before 1917 by a theorist almost unknown outside his native Hungary: Ernö Szontágh (Ervin Szabó).[1]

The son of middle-class Jewish parents, Szabó (1877–1918) attended the University of Vienna from 1899 to 1903 as a student of history and philosophy, made the acquaintance of Russian exiles living in Vienna, and became a Marxist, but also nourished his mind on the writings of Proudhon, Nietzsche, Lavrov, and Kropotkin. On his return to Budapest he was entrusted by the leaders of the Socialist Party with the edition of a three-volume selection from the writings of Marx and Engels. From 1905 onward he set himself publicly in opposition to the rather philistine leadership of Hungarian Social Democracy, speaking out against its bureaucratic habits and its complacent trust in evolution, and opposing to its rather somnolent passivity the anarchosyndicalist doctrines then brought to prominence in France by radical labor leaders who envisaged the proletarian revolution in the image of a general strike. Anarchosyndicalism was an eclectic doctrine which drew simultaneously on Marx, Proudhon, Sorel, and Bakunin. In France it had a following among the working class and was officially adopted by the principal union organization, the Con-

[1] See Peter Ludz, "Der Begriff der 'demokratischen Diktatur' in der politischen Philosophie von Georg Lukács," in *Georg Lukács—Festschrift zum 80. Geburtstag*, pp. 39 ff. See also the revised edition of this essay in *Georg Lukács—Schriften zur Ideologie und Politik*, where it figures as an editorial introduction. For the events of 1919 and Lukács' part in them, see Rudolf L. Tökés, *Béla Kun and the Hungarian Soviet Republic*.

fédération générale du travail, in the so-called Charte d'Amiens of October 1906. In Hungary it was resisted not only by the Socialist Party but by the unions, making converts chiefly among students and other intellectuals. Since in pre-1914 Austria-Hungary these members of the intelligentsia were mainly of Jewish origin, what began as a theoretical dispute was gradually envenomed by racial animosities, as well as by the natural distrust felt by down-to-earth labor organizers for loquacious intellectuals from the middle class. The resulting mutual dislikes were further inflamed in 1918 and 1919, the leadership of the newly founded Hungarian Communist Party being largely made up of intellectuals, whom the Social Democrats held responsible for the disaster of the brief Soviet experiment and the ensuing bloody persecution of Socialists and Communists alike by the triumphant "White" counter-revolution. Szabó, who had died in September 1918, did not live to witness the unsuccessful attempt to stage a repetition of Lenin's seizure of power, nor was he able to acknowledge his own appointment to an honorary membership in the Moscow Socialist Academy. His position as chief theorist of the Hungarian ultra-left was inherited by Lukács.[2]

The socialist student club founded by Szabó in 1902, self-styled the Revolutionary Socialist Students of Budapest, counted Lukács among its charter members.

[2] For details see Tökés, *op. cit.*, pp. 9 ff., 30 ff., 53 ff., 91 ff., 123 ff. Victor Zitta, who devotes a good deal of space to Lukács' activities as Deputy Commissar for Education and even lists the salary scale he drew up for the payment of stagehands and theatrical decorators (*Georg Lukács' Marxism*, pp. 98 ff.), is rather vague about his crucially important allegiance to an ultra-leftist faction whose outlook in 1919 was anarchosyndicalist rather than Leninist. The group included József Révai, the arch-Stalinist dictator of Hungary's cultural life after 1945 and by then Lukács' principal opponent within the party.

Around 1910 those of its former adherents who had not left Hungary for Germany frequented the lectures organized by a rather less militant organization, the Galileo Circle. This latter group was founded in the fall of 1908 with a charter membership of 256 to represent student interests and to provide a forum for educational activities within the university. Its inaugural statement affirmed that the Circle, "fully aware of the historic mission of the intellectuals . . . resolves to unify and strengthen the intellectual resources of Hungarian students . . . thus enabling them to become one day resolute, well-equipped, and conscious fighters for the social emancipation of Hungary." To this end the Circle promoted democratic and anticlerical campaigns of a kind that left-wing liberals would naturally support, especially in a country such as Hungary whose antiquated system of government, although parliamentary in form, was anything but democratic. The Circle also arranged lectures and seminars on contemporary philosophy, sociology, history, and aesthetics, distinguished guest speakers including Eduard Bernstein and the Viennese Marxist scholar Max Adler. Although never grouping more than a few hundred students, it thus provided a forum for the public expression of views which by local standards were certainly radical, if not exactly subversive. Most of its adherents could fairly have been described as radical liberals, but they overlapped with the small anarchosyndicalist group of which Szabó had become the theoretical inspirer. Neither organization obtained any encouragement from the Hungarian Social Democratic Party, which was busy organizing the workers, and whose leaders placed their trust in Karl Kautsky's determinist interpretation of Marxism. It was his revulsion against the complacency of this Social Democratic orthodoxy that had induced Szabó to espouse syndicalism. Others—including the future Communist theorist László Rudas—also conflicted sharply with the official leadership, and the youthful journalist Gyula Alpári, after various abortive rebellions, was actually expelled from the Party (a decision subsequently ratified by the 1910 Copenhagen Congress of the Socialist International, with Lenin and Rosa Luxemburg dissenting). To no one's surprise Alpári emerged in February 1919 as a prize convert to the Hungarian Communist Party.[3]

While Lukács was not involved in these purely political matters, he kept in touch with Szabó, who in his eyes represented what was alive and valuable in the socialist tradition. Hence his later apologetic references to Sorel, whose writings formed part of Szabó's ideological equipment. Hence also the key role which the notion of "consciousness" began to assume in his thinking. What this concept then signified to the Budapest intellectuals may be inferred from a letter addressed to Szabó by Oszkár Jászi, the distinguished editor of an influential liberal-radical journal, *Huszadik Század* (*Twentieth Century*), which had appropriately made its debut on January 1, 1900: "We intellectuals must work to transform that which lives half-consciously in the masses into an integral world view, and to undermine the existing society with [the] weapons of morality, science and the arts." There was nothing specifically socialist, let alone Marxist, about this pronouncement— save for the emphasis upon the key role of the intellectuals in articulating the consciousness of the masses.

[3] Tökés, *op. cit.*, p. 15. The decisive step in transforming these left-wing Socialist and antimilitarist elements into the nucleus of a pro-Bolshevik opposition group within the Socialist Party was the formation in November 1918 of an "Ervin Szabó Circle" as a political club dedicated to the radicalization of socialist policies. This immediately preceded the formation of the Hungarian Communist Party.

Jászi, who on occasion borrowed from the syndicalist vocabulary, held that the basic issue in Hungary was landownership: a perfectly sensible belief which he shared with moderate democrats. Himself a socialist, he influenced Szabó, who in turn passed his notions on to Lukács. It is noteworthy that Szabó, in an article of 1903–1904 published in Kautsky's *Neue Zeit*, identified socialism with the struggle for freedom and, specifically, for what he called "the democratic world order." An ethical rigorist, Szabó eventually repudiated not only parliamentary politics but political compromise as such—a kind of moralism which until the seizure of power was compatible with the revolutionary fervor of the syndicalist movement. The problem of keeping the revolution "pure" and uncorrupted then assumed a different form.

But let us stay for a moment with Oszkár Jászi's journal. At the start this monthly publication had the backing of wealthy businessmen and lawyers, until the editor's hankering for socialism brought about a divorce which in turn had the effect of driving Jászi and his friends leftward in the direction of the labor movement. The journal had originally been launched to promote liberal democratic aims in a profoundly conservative country ruled by great landowners, the military, and the clergy. Within a year its editors had founded a Society for Social Science, which promptly became a forum for debates on the respective merits of Fabianism, Marxism, Syndicalism, and other intellectual novelties. The radicals, that is to say, discovered socialism and sociology at the same time. Most of them came from well-to-do homes and would have been quite content with liberalism—if only there had been the slightest chance of making it work in a country like Hungary, where democracy inevitably spelled revolution (for no one doubted that a democratic Republic would dispossess the great magnates who owned one-third of Hungary's soil and controlled parliament and the government). In this respect, at least, Hungary was more akin to Tsarist Russia than to Germany, let alone Western Europe. In principle a democratic transformation ought to have been acceptable to middle-class moderates, but those among them who had originally backed the venture soon withdrew their support. When they seceded, Jászi and his friends were left with no option: if they wanted to acquire a popular following they had to turn to the industrial proletariat. But for what purpose? In Marxist terms they were aiming at a "bourgeois revolution," even if their private convictions were socialist or syndicalist. This kind of ambiguity, very familiar in our time, was new to Hungarian intellectuals in 1910, although Russian and Polish radicals had been struggling for decades with the problems it entailed. Talk of raising the consciousness of the masses to that of the intellectual vanguard would have sounded familiar to Lenin and Rosa Luxemburg. Precisely for this reason, Lukács— like Szabó a contributor to *Twentieth Century*—had no great difficulty after 1917 in making the transition from Sorel to the revolutionary socialism of Rosa Luxemburg, and thereafter to Leninism.

And there was something else: the key role of the intellectuals inevitably translated itself into the doctrine that a moral reformation must precede political revolution. Jászi had described his journal as "an expression of a new spiritual and moral synthesis." Szabó—himself an associate editor of *Twentieth Century* and vice-chairman of the Society for Social Sciences—never tired of emphasizing the ethical impulse inherent in the original socialist message, and Lukács in 1920 devoted an essay to problems of Communist morality. Published in German, in *Kommunismus*, an organ of the Communist International then edited by him in Vienna, this article, "Die moralische Sendung der kommunistischen Partei," was the sequel to a rebuke Lukács had earned from Lenin[4] for an earlier contribution in which he called for a boycott of parliamentary elections. Lenin on this occasion sided with the Hungarian party leader Béla Kun (later shot on Stalin's orders in 1939) against the "ultra-leftist" Lukács, who in 1920 still conserved some remnants of his syndicalist faith. But this incident need not concern us here. What is of genuine interest is Lukács' definition of the Communist Party's "moral mission." The party, he wrote, "is the organizational expression of the proletariat's revolutionary will." This formulation—more in tune with Rosa Luxemburg's way of thinking than with Lenin's—harked back to those pre-1914 days when Lukács had invested his political faith in the anarchosyndicalist "decisionism" of Sorel and Szabó. The basic orientation underlying this kind of theorizing was quite compatible with the moralism he had imbibed in Heidelberg while he was the pupil and friend of Lask. That the role of consciousness (and of conscience) is decisive—that it is *not* an epiphenomenon of the "real" historical process—was a conviction all these thinkers had in common.

Given these assumptions, Szabó's disciple was able after 1917 to make the transition from Syndicalism to Bolshevism, once the Russian Revolution had offered the spectacle of workers' councils seemingly taking the place of bourgeois parliamentary institutions. That the Soviets were in fact controlled by Lenin's party (and in its absence would have fallen under the control of some

[4] Lenin, *Collected Works* (Moscow, 1966), XXXI, 165.

other political organization) was not then as obvious to Central European Marxists as it became a decade later, by which time Lukács had accepted Leninism and abandoned his Luxemburgist heresies.

Significantly, the intellectual turmoil set going in Hungary by the war also witnessed the rise of a different kind of elitism on the political Left: that of the technicians. The Social Democratic Party, and the unions it controlled, characteristically had made no effort to organize industrial engineers, scientists, draughtsmen, managerial staffs, and other white-collar workers. These members of what some writers would later characterize as the *Produktionsintelligenz* had been radicalized by the war, and in early 1917—spurred on by the opening phase of the Russian Revolution, before the Bolsheviks had taken over—they formed a union of their own, with the twofold aim of representing their corporate interests and helping the antiwar opposition already founded by youthful labor activists, Syndicalists, and dissident Socialists. Having been systematically ignored and snubbed by the slow-witted union leaders and the lethargic Social Democratic Party, these newly politicized technicians promptly invented a socialist ideology of their own, later known as "engineer socialism." Their principal theorist, Gyula Hevesi, may be said to have reinvented Saint-Simonism, although doubtless that was not how he saw it. In the words of a later Communist historian, he put forward

a plan to bring about a revolution by concerted sabotage action of technicians and engineers . . . destined to become the chief actors in social transformations. Hevesi rejected Marx's theory of surplus value. According to him, the major share of surplus value originated from engineering and technical inventions. . . .

The workers were to be . . . auxiliary allies in the battle of the "creative producers."[5]

Equipped with this technocratic faith, the left-wingers among the intelligentsia set to work, and by the end of 1917 made contact with Syndicalist labor organizers in Budapest, at the expense of the Social Democrats and the rather stodgy unions they controlled. At this stage they were joined by Marxist intellectuals who had emerged from the Galileo Circle, by Szabó and his followers among the students, and by prominent antiwar Socialists such as Ilona Duczynszka, recently arrived from Switzerland with propagandist literature supplied by Lenin's friend Angelica Balabanova. The resulting antiwar agitation among shop stewards already sympathetic to Syndicalist ideas became a factor in the dramatic events of 1918 and 1919, when the old regime in Hungary collapsed under the impact of military defeat abroad and popular unrest at home. With the break-up of the Austro-Hungarian Monarchy in November 1918, the stage was set for the brief experiment of the Hungarian Soviet Republic, after the liberal-socialist government of Count Mihály Károlyi (which included Oszkár Jászi, representing the bourgeois Radicals) had resigned on March 21, 1919, leaving the way free for the Social Democrats to set up a coalition government with the Communists—whose leaders were released from prison that very day, and took over as People's Commissars twenty-four hours later!

The share taken by Lukács in these dramatic events was not negligible. Returning to Budapest from Heidelberg in 1917—after an earlier stay in 1915 and 1916, when he was employed as a post office censor, a task we may assume he interpreted in a liberal spirit—he

[5] József Lengyel, cited by Tökés, *op. cit.*, p. 31.

joined the future sociologist Karl Mannheim and the art critic Arnold Hauser in a "Free School of the Humanities." This was an enterprise which fed the general stream of intelligentsia radicalism but had no party-political character. Lukács' own standpoint at the time has been described by those who knew him best as "Tolstoian ethical socialism."[6] Certainly he did not at once join the Communist Party founded in late November 1918, when the recently returned Kun insisted on a formal secession from the Socialists and eventually brought about a split—with the help of Syndicalist shop stewards, dissident Social Democrats, anarchist intellectuals, and Hevesi's "engineer socialists" (whose leader, notwithstanding his un-Marxist deviations, was coopted to the Central Committee on December 15). At some time during this month (the precise date is uncertain) Lukács, after initial hesitations, joined the Party, but he was not included in the self-appointed Central Committee, which was dominated by Kun's reliably Bolshevik group, plus four leading former Social Democrats, among whom László Rudas distinguished himself for many years by his unflinching Leninist-Stalinist orthodoxy. It is all the more remarkable that during the brief period in February and March of 1919 when Kun and his closest associates were in jail, Lukács—together with Tibor Szamuely, József Révai, Ernö Bettelheim, and Elek Bolgár—not only ran the underground "second Central Committee" then in control of the Party apparatus, but held it to an ultra-leftist course and joined the others in preparing for an armed rising in May. It would appear that the temporary absence of Kun and the other Moscow-trained leaders had released Lukács' anarcho-syndicalist longings, for the planned uprising—which never materialized, Károlyi having suddenly resigned

[6] *Ibid.*, p. 96.

and handed power to the Communists—was to have begun with a general strike and culminated in an armed insurrection and a brief period of terrorism. The hurriedly arranged Socialist-Communist merger which enabled Kun and his associates to form a coalition government quite peacefully on March 22 was not to the taste of these ultra-leftists who held that power had to be gained by violence. But Lukács bowed to party discipline and took his seat in the new government as Deputy Commissar for Education and nominal second-in-command of the veteran Social Democrat Zsigmond Kunfi.

The brief and disastrous episode of the Hungarian Soviet Republic enters into consideration here because it furnished Lukács with an arsenal of political and theoretical weapons in his subsequent lengthy and unsuccessful struggle against Kun's faction. Here it is worth stressing that this confrontation turned on the issue of "bourgeois democracy": always a sore point with Communists and notably so in a backward country such as Hungary where the peasantry predominated, and where in consequence even a united Socialist-Communist coalition could not seriously hope to win a legislative majority. This well-founded pessimism concerning the probable outcome of popular elections had been among the reasons why the Social Democrats in March 1919 reluctantly abandoned Károlyi and threw in their lot with the Communists. To put the matter in Leninist language, their leaders had come around to the view that in Hungary a bourgeois-democratic revolution entailed a brief interim period of "proletarian dictatorship."

There was, however, a more immediate and pressing problem. The collapse of the Austro-Hungarian Monarchy had left Hungary wide open to military intervention from Rumania, Czechoslovakia, and Serbia—all backed by the Western powers in general and France in particular. These countries had territorial claims upon the Hungarian half of the Dual Monarchy, for Hungary's rulers had for centuries lorded it not only over their own peasantry but over oppressed national minorities as well. The armistice agreement Károlyi had been obliged to sign on November 13, 1918, divested Hungary of about half its former territory. An ultimatum delivered by the French chairman of the Entente military mission in Budapest on March 19, ordering the Hungarian government to withdraw its troops behind new demarcation lines and threatening military action in case of non-compliance, did the rest. National feelings were aroused, and when Károlyi rejected the ultimatum and simultaneously released the jailed Communist leaders, the latter were able within forty-eight hours to assume power on a wave of far from artificial patriotic and popular sentiment. The Socialist leader Sándor Garbai set the tone by telling the Budapest Workers' Council on March 20, "We must take a new direction to obtain from the East what has been denied us by the West. We must join the stream of new events. The army of the Russian proletariat is approaching rapidly." It was in this spirit that the short-lived Hungarian Soviet Republic sought to amalgamate socialism and nationalism during the five months of its existence. When in August it was overthrown by the "White" army of Admiral Horthy, helped by Rumanian and Polish forces, the ensuing bloodbath far exceeded anything the Communists had permitted themselves in the way of terrorism during their brief tenure of power. In the words of a prominent and very moderate Social Democrat, who had been War Minister in Károlyi's government before assuming command of the Hungarian Red Army, "After the collapse of the revolution, the counterrevolutionaries reckoned up 234 victims of the revolutionary terror. As against this, they murdered 5000 revolutionaries within a few months."[7]

This was not the end of the matter. The Horthy regime, apart from executing five thousand men and women and jailing seventy-five thousand for alleged complicity with the Communists, also drove some hundred thousand people into emigration. The majority were liberal intellectuals and urban middle-class Jews, who had formed the backbone of whatever democratic life had existed in Hungary before the White terror. There occurred a notable exodus of distinguished scholars and artists holding no pronounced political views. Against the background of this cultural catastrophe, Lukács' activities as Deputy Commissar for Education (later as Commissar after his Socialist chief had left the government) hardly merit the attention they have received. There was neither time nor opportunity for more than a few utopian decrees intended to "raise the consciousness of the masses." What the Socialist intel-

[7] Wilhelm Böhm, *Im Kreuzfeuer zweier Revolutionen* (Munich, 1924), p. 445. Böhm makes the interesting point that Kun and other leading Communists spent a good deal of their time issuing exit visas to prominent members of the Hungarian aristocracy, so as to get them out of harm's way. At the same time they sanctioned the shooting of hostages and other ill-judged and quite unnecessary acts of terrorism, thereby antagonizing their Socialist allies and speeding their own downfall. It was the 1871 Paris Commune all over again, with a refinement the Moscow-trained group among the Communist leaders had learned from their Bolshevik teachers: the setting up of something like a Hungarian imitation of the Cheka, headed by one Otto Korvin, who proved an able practitioner in this field. "The institution of early-morning preventive arrests, torture chambers in the basement of the parliament building, and the holding of hostages from among suspected counterrevolutionaries were Korvin's contributions to the cause of the Hungarian proletarian revolution." Tökés, *op. cit.*, pp. 158–59.

lectuals thought of their Communist allies may be inferred from this recollection of one of their surviving leaders:

> They were philosophers, poets and aesthetes who stepped into the healthy storm of the revolution, but they could not take the continuous fights . . . and in the end they sullenly slipped back to the lukewarm bottomless mud of their doctrinaire fixed ideas. Dangers abounded outside, but they gathered . . . in the Soviet House, and the endless bitter debates began. There was György Lukács, the former Heidelberg philosopher, József Révai, former bank clerk and aesthete . . . Ervin Sinkó, the young Christian Tolstoyan writer . . . and Elena Andreevna Grabenko, Lukács' Russian wife. There were also some scatterbrained ideologues. Quotations from Hegel, Marx, Kierkegaard, Fichte, Weber, Jean Paul, Hölderlin, and Novalis were flying in the air.[8]

It is a testimony to the reputation Lukács had acquired during his Heidelberg period that his arrest in Vienna, in October 1919, at the instigation of the new Hungarian regime, evoked a successful campaign on his behalf in which Thomas Mann and other German literary notables took the lead. Following his release a few months later, he plunged into the factional disputes then raging among the Communist refugees in Vienna, where the illegal Hungarian party had established a bureau. (It was in the course of these internal debates that he

---

[8] Lajos Kassák, cited by Tökés, *op. cit.*, p. 197. Kassák is not perhaps the most impartial of witnesses. As editor of the radical literary journal *Today* he had earlier refused to publish a nihilistic poem by Révai for which the future arch-Stalinist—then a flaming anarchist—had chosen the eloquent title "My Mother, My Father, My First Teacher: You Should Die like a Dog." As a result, Révai broke with the group and with Kassák. For this episode see Tökés, *op. cit.*, p. 96n.

worked out the doctrines put forward in the celebrated essay collection *History and Class Consciousness*.) Lukács' political and theoretical line during the 1920s was determined by this struggle, whose full significance was disclosed to the world only in 1956, when the brief Hungarian "thaw" permitted him to acquaint the public with his involvement in it. During those years, he had become a close ally of Jenö Landler, a prominent survivor of the 1919 catastrophe and Kun's rival for the leadership of the Hungarian Communist Party. In 1928 and 1929 Lukács committed himself to an action program—the so-called "Blum theses" (Blum being Lukács' "party name" within the illegal Hungarian Communist organization)—wherein he developed a political standpoint of his own. After Landler's death in 1928 and the subsequent rejection of his "theses" by the Moscow-centered Hungarian leaders and by the Communist International itself, he was excluded from all decision-making processes and obliged—much against his inclination—to confine himself to philosophy and literary criticism.[9]

What the heretical "Blum theses" put forward was a radical-democratic platform centered on the idea that the Horthy regime could only be replaced by a democratic republic. From this it followed that the perspective of a "proletarian dictatorship" in the Bolshevik sense had to be abandoned, if only because Landler and Lukács aimed at an alliance with the Social Democrats (who had once more been legalized and, within limits, permitted to resume their activities). Although couched in Leninist language, the "Blum theses" were an attempt to work out the strategy of a democratic revolution which in its later stages might, but need not, lead

[9] For Lukács' account, see *Georg Lukács—Schriften zur Literatur und Politik*, pp. 763 ff.

towards socialism—provided genuine popular support could be obtained for measures directed against private property. To an extent, then, Lukács' "right-wing deviation" of this time was part of a wider factional struggle associated with the name of Nikolai Bukharin (1888–1938), who then challenged Stalin's plunge into terrorism at home and left-wing adventurism abroad. It is not without interest that, speaking in 1956 after Khrushchev's well-known denunciation of Stalin, Lukács failed to invoke the authority of Bukharin, the most prominent victim of the 1936–1938 Moscow trials. His own "Bukharinism" in 1928 and 1929 had wrecked his political career, but he conserved both his party membership and the right to interpret Marxism-Leninism for the benefit of his German and Hungarian readers, on the understanding that he would not intervene in political matters. Nor did he, until the "thaw" of 1956 encouraged him to resume his vendetta against Kun and simultaneously to announce that his withdrawal of the "Blum theses" in 1929 had been induced by purely tactical considerations.

Before going into the details of Lukács' celebrated heresy in 1923 let us note that his general orientation during those years clashed with Lenin's understanding of philosophy, for in recovering the Hegelian dimension of Marx's thought, he had unwittingly transgressed upon Lenin's version of Engels' "dialectical materialism," with its naïvely pictorial interpretation of the role of consciousness. At the same time he sought to reconcile Lenin's elitist view of the Communist Party's role with his own residual faith in Rosa Luxemburg and syndicalism. Philosophically speaking, he appeared to his Leninist critics as a left-wing Hegelian rather than as a materialist. Yet he allotted to the role of revolutionary "consciousness" an importance quite consonant with

Lenin's own conception of politics. The ascription to the proletariat (in practice to the Communist Party as the "vanguard" of this movement) of a viewpoint radically different from that of bourgeois society furnished him with a criterion for his definition of ideology: he attributed "false consciousness" uniquely to the self-definition of the ruling class, while crediting the submerged revolutionary class with the possession of a "true consciousness," albeit imperfectly articulated and thus necessitating the guidance of the Communist Party.[10]

The term "vanguard"—with its implication that it was simply a matter of forcing the pace and giving battle at a point in time chosen in advance of circumstances visible to the whole movement—concealed a crucial difficulty: the Party was not in fact the most forward section of the proletarian army at all, but a "classless" force

[10] For the moral implications of this doctrine, see Franz Borkenau, *The Communist International*, pp. 172–73. Elitism, when given this kind of philosophical sanction, usually leads to the doctrine that the elect are free to disregard the moral constraints they impose upon others. For the rest, the adherents of this new esoteric wisdom could find in Dostoevski some useful hints about the dialectic whereby an infallible authority justifies its monopoly of control.

In March 1921, Ilona Duczynska, by then an apostate from the Leninist faith, described Lukács' esoteric doctrine as follows in the German Socialist publication *Unser Weg*, then edited by Rosa Luxemburg's former colleague and successor, Paul Levi: "A representative theoretican, who was perhaps the sole brain behind Hungarian Communism, at a decisive moment answered my question as to whether lying and cheating of party members by their own leaders were admissible by this statement: Communist ethics make it the highest duty to accept the necessity of acting wickedly. This, he said, was the greatest sacrifice the revolution demanded from us. . . . This dialectical doctrine . . . has never been published by the theorist in question, but . . . it spread as a secret doctrine . . . until it was finally regarded as the semi-official quintessence of true communism." In the light of this curious utterance, Lukács' unflinching adherence to Stalin need occasion no great surprise.

which had imposed itself upon an immature labor movement. This was not at all what Marx had in mind when he told the workers they would get nowhere without an adequate awareness of their ultimate aims. In the Marxian perspective, the emancipation of the working class is the business of that class itself, and not of a revolutionary elite of intellectuals. The class no doubt has varying levels of consciousness, and Socialists are called upon to work with the most advanced; but that is all. An elite which embodies a consciousness denied to the class is a concept that Marx would not have accepted. In practice Lenin did not formulate the matter quite so clearly. That was left to outsiders like Lukács, who for this reason had to be cold-shouldered. Many leading Communists themselves did not then realize to what they were committed. Moreover, they could and did point out that Lukács was philosophically a heretic in that he was a left-wing Hegelian rather than a materialist. Yet so far as his politics were concerned, their embarrassment sprang from the fact that he had gone further than Lenin in making explicit the inherent implications of the new status allotted to the Party: the kind of Marxism he postulated had an elitist ring. With its elevation of the "vanguard" to the role of an independent historical entity which alone embodied the true consciousness of the revolution, Lukács' version of Leninism had become incompatible with Rosa Luxemburg's romantic exaltation of the mass movement.

Paradoxically, Lukács, by exalting the historical role of a working class which in actual fact was not revolutionary in his sense of the term, prepared the ground for the subsequent Stalinist discovery that the proletariat was a counter-revolutionary class which must be held down by force. The full implications of this state of affairs burst upon the world at the time of the Hungarian uprising in 1956, when Lukács—not for the first time—gave evidence of personal inconsistency in that he halfheartedly sided with the rebels, thus repudiating the implications of his own elitism.

This, however, was not quite the end of the matter. In the later 1960s, Lukács' old acquaintance András Hegedus—a former associate of Rákosi and as such Prime Minister of Hungary from April 1955 to October 1956—ran into trouble with the post-Stalin and post-Rákosi leadership of the Party by putting forward some extremely heretical notions of his own which raised the specter of a different kind of elitism: strictly technocratic and recalling Hevesi's ideas about "engineer socialism" in 1917–1918. Among others he advanced the following theses:

1. Sociology—indeed the whole of scientific and scholarly endeavor—cannot be the servant of any party or political creed. The constant search for truth is its only goal.

2. Conflicts among interest groups in a socialist society are not only legitimate but beneficial, provided that institutional forms are created for their resolution. The proper role of a trade union, for example, is the protection of workers' rights.

3. Marxist theory contains a number of myths whose sole function is to galvanize the proletariat into revolutionary action. Once consolidated, however, the regime should confront these myths with reality lest they harden into dogma, as under Rákosi. To this end, the social sciences (especially sociology) should be free to criticize all aspects of society.[11]

---

[11] See "Hegedus: His Views and His Critics," in *Studies in Comparative Communism* (Los Angeles), April 1969, pp. 121 ff. The heresies in question made their appearance in various semiofficial party publications from 1964 on, when their

For good measure Hegedus affirmed that democracy was becoming a real problem under socialism. Writing in June 1968, when democratic forces in neighboring Czechoslovakia seemed on the verge of scoring a political triumph, Hegedus had this to say:

The Leninist party evolved in the struggle with reformist trends and also with revisionist Social-Democratic parties, as the leading party in the struggle for the rule of the working class and in the battle fought by the workers to achieve this aim. The object was to attain a domination which should put an end to the right of private ownership of capital, and to all those institutional forms of capitalist authority and power which were built on private ownership or were intended for its protection at all costs. No one who does not weigh up carefully this historic function of the Leninist party, with all its consequences, is really able to understand anything of the lessons to be drawn from our most recent history.

With the creation of the power of the working class, a new situation arose: the party struggling for power became the party in power with, again, both positive and negative consequences. (This new function created a particularly difficult situation for those parties which, as a result of peculiarities in the historic situation, became strong organizations qualified to lead the masses only in this second phase.) Possibilities opened up for solving the new tasks in various ways, but one thing was unavoidable: in one form or another a system of state administration of a new type had to be constructed and stabilized, namely civic discipline,

author was chairman of the editorial board of *Valosag*, a socio-political monthly published by the Society for the Propagation of Scientific Knowledge, a post from which he was duly removed in August 1965, by which time the former arch-Stalinist had become an out-and-out revisionist. He continued, however, to spread his appalling doctrines in other journals until late 1968.

which, as far as the subject we are discussing was concerned, meant that real power had to be given to the most varied management administrations. . . .

Three alternatives . . . were advanced in the years immediately after the victory of the socialist revolution. . . .

The first was elaborated by Trotsky, who was the protagonist of the creation of a monolithic state on a military model (let no one be led astray by the fact that in the thirties Trotsky was the most violent critic of the solution which he himself had been the first to formulate in theory but which was put into actual practice under Stalin's leadership).

The supporters of the second alternative are the representatives of the so-called workers' opposition: what they want is that at the most varied levels of economic direction the workers, or rather the trade unions as the workers' representatives, should elect the economic leaders (from foreman to people's commissar). They stand for the committee method, for "collective leadership" in opposition to responsible leadership by individuals. . . .

I find myself in the most difficult position when I come to . . . the third alternative; in part it seems to me unequivocally demonstrated that Lenin perceived—even if he did not formulate it in this way— the difference between management power and the authority of society; yet on the other hand, I am far from believing that Lenin saw everything correctly. . . .

Yet Lenin did see two important things—although he was not destined to find time to elaborate the theory of the socialist state—and the first thing was that in the socialist state there would necessarily and inevitably evolve management systems in which bureaucratic conditions in the Marxist sense would again be created; and that the socialist society would have to do everything possible to bring about their control by the ordinary workers—by which he meant in essence those doing direct manual labor. He was far from acknowledging this controlling function to be the privilege of *individuals*: he wanted to draw *everyone* into the social control of management, to teach *everyone* how to perform this function.

The author of these lines had traveled a long distance from the simple faith of the first generation of Hungarian Communists. Let us now return to the formulation that faith was given by Lukács after he had made the transition from "ultra-leftism" to Leninism.

History and Class Consciousness

●

IV

In the preceding chapters we have encountered some of the major crosscurrents whose confluence turned Vienna for a brief period into the intellectual capital of Central Europe. In engaging the topic of Lukács' first major work in Marxist theory we descend into a whirlpool. It is perhaps worth reminding ourselves at this stage that Vienna likewise gave birth to psychoanalysis and logical positivism, and that Lukács was not influenced by either. If in later years he took note of Freud, it was to deplore what he termed his "irrationalism"—a judgment not shared by the influential Marxists of the Frankfurt school, which constituted itself in the 1930s. As for logical positivism, the convert to Hegel could see in it only the inevitable outcome of the neo-Kantian orthodoxy he had already repudiated before 1914. In terms of intellectual history, it may nonetheless be of some significance that the publication of *History and Class Consciousness* (1923) very nearly coincided with the printed appearance of Ludwig Wittgenstein's *Tractatus* (1922). In both cases, the author—rendered famous by a radical departure from the prevailing orthodoxy in his respective domain—was in later years to renounce the work that had fired the imagination of his contemporaries. But there the resemblance ends. Although both were raised in the shadow of the decaying Habsburg Monarchy and affected by the strains inherent in a collapsing culture, two more different characters than Georg Lukács and Ludwig Wittgenstein it would be difficult to imagine.

History and Class Consciousness, it has been said with truth, owes its enduring relevance to the manner in which Lukács recaptured the Hegelian dimension of Marx's thought. The explosive effect it produced within the European Communist movement was due to simpler considerations. The Communist International had only recently embarked upon the lengthy and arduous task of "Bolshevizing" its various national sections: that is to say, of transforming a motley army of erstwhile pacifists, anarchosyndicalists, and rebellious left-wing socialists into disciplined Leninists. From the standpoint of Lenin's heirs—held together by little save veneration for the leader who lay paralyzed in the Kremlin after his second stroke in March 1923, ten months before death ended his mute torment—nothing could have been less welcome than the sudden emergence of a specifically "Western" school of Communism, represented by theorists such as Lukács, the German philosophy professor Karl Korsch, and the Italian Marxist Antonio Graziadei. The torrent of abuse that descended upon Lukács in 1923 and 1924 is in part explicable in terms of factional animosities. But the principal source of this hysteria was the mentality of the Russian Communists, for whom Lenin had become a sacred icon. Any "deviation" from what was now described as "Marxism-Leninism" constituted an affront to their faith and simultaneously raised the terrifying specter of uncontrollable heresies sprouting among Communists who had not been properly Bolshevized. The struggle against Lukács "on the philosophical front" thus became a major occupation for such Soviet philosophers as A. M. Deborin, I. Luppol, G. Bammel, and other exegetes of Lenin, but the political leaders were drawn in too. At the fifth Comintern congress in Moscow, in June and July of 1924, Bukharin —since Lenin's death the Russian Party's leading spokesman on all theoretical matters—contented himself with a brief remark deploring recent "relapses into the old Hegelianism." His colleague Zinoviev, a vain and foolish demagogue whose mental equipment hardly fitted him for his exalted role, poured out his wrath over "ultra-leftists" who somehow were likewise "revisionists," invoked the sacred name of Lenin, sneered at "professors" such as Korsch, Lukács, and Graziadei, and solemnly declared that their aberrations could not be tolerated.

What made the whole affair so embarrassing was that Lukács in his book had established a somewhat artificial connection between Lenin and Rosa Luxemburg: the latter a revolutionary saint since her murder by German officers in January 1919, but also a former ally of the Mensheviks and a critic of Bolshevik principles and practices. In 1924 "Luxemburgism" was not yet a major heresy, nor had "Trotskyism" raised its head (in any case Lukács never professed the faintest sympathy for Trotsky). But an "ultra-leftist" current did exist among Western Communists of syndicalist origin who could not quite stomach the notion that workers' councils were there only for the purpose of ratifying the party's decrees. Lukács' intellectual development—from the anarchosyndicalism of Szabó to the revolutionary socialism of Luxemburg, and then to Lenin—made him dangerous, and the political message of his 1923 publication, for all his copious references to Lenin, could be interpreted in a sense unwelcome from the authoritarian Bolshevik standpoint.

By comparison with the latent menace of political "deviation," the rather esoteric issues involved in Lukács' more theoretical essays did not weigh heavily in the balance, save in so far as he ventured to criticize Engels' handling of certain logical and epistemological concepts. For this awkward topic impinged directly upon Leninism as a philosophy, inasmuch as Lenin's only major work in this field, *Materialism and Empiriocriticism*, committed his followers to Engels' "dialectical materialism": so described by the "founder of Russian Marxism," G. V. Plekhanov (1856–1918), for whom in his capacity as a theorist Lenin always retained the highest respect. Soviet Marxism, on its philosophical side, was and is rooted in Plekhanov and Lenin. Both were rigid adherents of what in those days passed for orthodox Marxism: meaning the codification of Marx's thought worked out by Engels after the death of his senior partner. When therefore Lukács in 1923 came forward with a highly original interpretation which cast doubt upon Engels' understanding of Kant and Hegel (and, by implication, Marx), the rage of the orthodox—in Central Europe as well as in the U.S.S.R.—knew no bounds. They were no less infuriated by Korsch, whose *Marxismus und Philosophie* likewise treated materialism in general, and "dialectical materialism" in particular, as a naïve attempt to revert to a pre-Kantian standpoint. As Lukács, Korsch, and their adherents saw the matter, Marxism was indeed—as Engels had affirmed in his influential essay on Ludwig Feuerbach in 1888—the inheritor of classical German philosophy. But precisely for this reason it was incumbent upon Marxists to avoid a relapse into "pre-critical"—i.e., pre-Kantian—thinking. In so far as Engels had, here and there, yielded to this temptation, Lukács—secure in the knowledge that he had fully assimilated the meaning of Kant's and Hegel's philosophy during his prewar years in Heidelberg—felt obliged to correct him. *History and Class Consciousness* bore the subtitle *Studies in Marxist Dialectics*: in itself a plain enough indication that its author desired to have no truck with "materialism." But the really flagrant offense went beyond this. Lukács not merely questioned Engels' understanding of Kant and Hegel: he actually went so far as to describe the old materialism of the Enlightenment as "the ideological form of the bourgeois revolution."[1]

In order to perceive why this seemingly harmless phrase struck Russian and Central European Communists with the force of a bombshell one has to grasp the philosophical and political connection between the French and the Russian revolutions. Lenin's entire world-view centered upon an assimilation of French eighteenth-century materialism, of which Marxism appeared to him to represent the contemporary form.

[1] For this and the following see *Geschichte und Klassenbewusstsein*. The crucial passages relating to Engels' misinterpretation of Kant and Hegel are on pages 311 ff. and 387 ff. of the 1968 edition in the *Werke*, and the characterization of philosophical materialism—i.e., the materialism of Holbach and Helvetius, and the French Encyclopaedists in general—as "the ideological form of the bourgeois revolution" occurs in a footnote on p. 390. All the relevant passages are found in the lengthy essay "Die Verdinglichung und das Bewusstsein des Proletariats," which makes up the centerpiece of the book.

While on occasion—e.g., in his "philosophical note-books" of 1914 to 1916, first published in 1932—he praised Hegel's *Logic*, of which he had by then made a fairly thorough study, he seems never to have grasped the incompatibility of Hegel's dialectical method with the doctrinaire materialism on which he had been brought up. Kant in particular was anathema to him, and Engels' rather inadequate treatment of Kant in his essay on Feuerbach sufficed to persuade him—like Plekhanov before him—that Kant (and Fichte) need not be taken seriously. Lukács, having gone through the severe training of the neo-Kantian school before turning to Hegel, knew better. What he did not realize was that in venturing into this area he had unwittingly struck at the very core of Leninism as a world-view. For Lenin, as for other Russian Marxists of his persuasion, Kant represented a standing menace because his "agnostic-ism" concerning the existence of a "real world" inde-pendent of the mind seemingly opened a back door to "fideism," i.e., religion. If the mind did not portray the world as it really was, if there was an unknowable something—a "thing-in-itself" to employ the Kantian term—then might not idealist metaphysicians claim that empirical science was a necessary fiction? And once this was conceded, might not theology creep back? It is true that Lenin modified his standpoint to the extent of con-ceding that human consciousness was not passive. But he never really abandoned the transcript theory of cog-nition to which he had earlier committed himself, and above all he went on insisting upon the crucial impor-tance of "dialectical materialism" as a philosophy of nature. Materialism had to furnish an all-embracing explanation of the universe—how else could it take the place of revealed religion and idealist metaphysics? Thus when Lukács denied that Marxism had any bearing on natural science, he removed the keystone from the Leninist construction. And when he cited his old teacher Heinrich Rickert to the effect that materialism was "inverted Platonism,"[2] he laid sacrilegious hands upon the very ark of the covenant. As for his description of materialism as "bourgeois," it was only too plain that every "ultra-leftist" in Europe might draw the most alarming inferences concerning the "proletarian" character of the Russian revolution.

Compared to these explosive topics, Lukács' reservations about Engels' understanding of Kant were relatively harmless, albeit damaging since they came from a trained philosopher who was also a Marxist. Engels had in 1888 indeed adopted a quite untenable position. In his eagerness to refute Hume's and Kant's "philosophical crochets" concerning the cognition of reality, he had appealed to "experiment and industry" as proof that exhaustive knowledge of the actual world was possible.[3] As Lukács reasonably observed, this wholly missed the point of Kant's phenomenalism, which did not in any way cast doubt upon the possibility of a limitless advance in scientific knowledge. Kant had asserted something quite different: namely, that even the most complete understanding of all the natural phenomena present to the mind could not overcome the built-in dilemma inherent in man's thinking: the fact that he perceives the world with the help of a mental apparatus which imposes its own forms (the categories) upon the raw material of experience. The misunderstanding had arisen from Engels' failure to follow Hegel along a path that led back to the metaphysical rationalism of the

[2] *Ibid.*, p. 390.
[3] "Ludwig Feuerbach and the End of Classical German Philosophy," in Marx-Engels, *Selected Works* (London, 1968), p. 605.

Greeks (and of Spinoza), a rationalism which credited Reason with the power to comprehend the veritable nature of reality. If this was excluded, then the choice lay between Kant's phenomenalism and the positivism of the natural and social sciences, a positivism which refused to accept the distinction between phenomena and noumena, "things-for-us" and "things-in-themselves." Alternatively one might revert to the "naïve realism" of the scholastics, for whom the entire problem did not exist. In later years some Catholic philosophers were indeed to treat Thomism and Leninism as potential allies against Hegelianism, positivism, and Kantianism alike.[4] Scholastic realism and dialectical materialism after all both affirmed the existence of an objective world independent of the mind. Whatever one may think of this doctrine, it has a respectable pedigree going back all the way to Aristotle. If the Soviet philosophers had been solely concerned with problems of cognition, Lukács' heresies need not have given them sleepless nights.

But of course there was more to it. "Materialism" has a double meaning. It may be taken to signify the reality of the external world, but for Engels it also meant something else: the primacy of "matter" as an absolute substance involved in the constitution of the universe. Materialism in *this* sense is not a theory of knowledge, but a metaphysical doctrine about the world. It affirms that matter (or nature) is prior to spirit, or that spirit is an emanation of matter. Such affirmations can be neither proved nor disproved. Their acceptance resolves itself into an act of religious (or antireligious) faith. When Engels declared that he and Marx had adopted "materialism" as against Hegel's "idealism," what he meant was not that he and Marx held a theory of knowl-

[4] See Gustav A. Wetter, *Dialectical Materialism* (London and New York, 1958), passim.

edge different from Hegel's, but that they regarded "matter" as in some sense more fundamental than "spirit." Whether Marx ever actually said anything of the sort is a question that need not concern us here, but Engels certainly did hold such a view, whereas Lukács in 1923 did not.

What Lukács put forward in the central sections of *History and Class Consciousness* was a genuinely dialectical theory which undercut the stale dispute between materialists and spiritualists. His standpoint could be summarized by saying that materialism and spiritualism are the thesis and antithesis of a debate which has its origin in a failure to overcome the cleavage between subject and object. The solution lies not in opting for one or the other, but in transcending the area of dispute, and this can be done by following Marx in treating practice as the concrete union of thought and reality.

In advancing these notions, Lukács pioneered into virgin territory so far as his Marxist contemporaries were concerned, while at the same time he revived a mode of thought embedded in classical German philosophy. It is necessary to be clear as to what exactly this implied. His critics pounced upon what they termed his Hegelianism, while at the same time they upheld the thoroughly Hegelian approach inherent in Engels' later writings, notably his *Dialectics of Nature*. There was an element of insincerity about their posturing as defenders of materialist orthodoxy, for the more literate among them could not be unaware that the notion of a natural dialectic had been extracted by Engels from the *Logic* of the arch-idealist Hegel. In thus reverting to Hegel, Engels revived the Romantic project of a "philosophy of nature." Whether it makes sense for a materialist to pursue this train of thought is a question on which even Leninists are notoriously divided. The more sophisticated among them nowadays tend to edge away from attempts to construct an all-embracing ontology. Any such enterprise involves a return to the Hegelian notion that "being" and "consciousness" are ultimately identical. If this is so, it makes sense to read an element of self-awareness back into nature, but in that case materialism in the strict sense has been abandoned. Hence those among Lukács' critics who in 1923 and 1924 assailed him for introducing idealist concepts into Marxism were, to put it mildly, being a trifle inconsistent.

This circumstance, however, does not touch upon the theoretical core of the dispute. For while both sides were operating with arguments drawn from Marx and Hegel, there was a decisive difference in their respective understanding of what this intellectual heritage implied. For the Soviet philosophers, Marxism signified a "scientific" theory of socialism, in the sense which the term "science" had acquired between 1880 and 1920 for Engels, Kautsky, and other representatives of Social Democratic orthodoxy: a theoretical approach grounded in the distinction—familiar to every scientist—between the "real" world of objective "fact," and the subjective notions entertained by individuals about the reality confronting them. For anyone brought up in this tradition it went without saying that "science" recognized a radical cleavage between hard, solid, brute fact, and speculative daydreaming. In this respect there was no basic difference between Engels' Social Democratic pupils and the Soviet Marxists, for all that Lenin had written Kautsky off as a hopeless philistine. Lenin's activism was confined to politics; neither his belated discovery of Hegel in 1914–1916 nor his private urge to give "history" an occasional push had made a dent in his fundamental scientism. Theory for him was one thing, practice another; and practice, to be effective, had to insert itself into the sort of causally determined process that was supposed to operate in nature and history alike.

To be sure, there were historic opportunities that might be seized or missed, and it was the Party's task to mold circumstances, not to wait passively for the world to shape itself in accordance with the heart's desire. To that extent Lenin introduced a dialectical element into the theory and practice of revolutionary politics. The role of *consciousness* as the decisive factor in determining the outcome of political conflict was no longer obscured by the kind of Darwinian evolutionism which Kautsky (following Engels) had substituted for the Marxian "union of theory and practice." Kautsky's persistent waffling about "historical laws" (which he conceived on the model of the natural sciences) had in the end provoked a general rebellion that precipitated radical Socialists into the Bolshevik camp, just as it drove the former Sorelian Mussolini and his friends into Fascist irrationalism and elitism. But Lenin's partial return to Hegel—itself induced by the catastrophe of 1914 and the collapse of the Second International— stopped short of that radical renunciation of positivism which Lukács proposed in *History and Class Consciousness.* Not only did eighteenth-century French materialism continue to supply the philosophical foundation of Lenin's world-view: his insistence on the crucial role of consciousness had no philosophical consequences. What emerged from the crucible of the revolutionary years from 1917 to 1923 was the concept of an omniscient vanguard equipped with a "scientific" understanding of history: the Communist Party. Being in possession of veritable insight into the (inevitable) march of history, the Party had the duty to galvanize the proletariat into revolutionary action, whenever the situation called for it. All it needed for this purpose was a correct appreciation of what in Communist parlance came to be known as "the subjective factor," meaning the level of political awareness. For the rest, its leaders required organizational means to set the masses in motion, and these were duly supplied by the apparatus. So far from "the Party" viewing its relationship to "the class" as a mere "moment" within a dialectical totality, it was supposed to incarnate the true self-consciousness of the epoch. By the same token its leaders had to appear infallible, and in the end they became the prisoners of their own mythology.

What Lukács in 1923 opposed to this mechanical disjunction between the subject of history (the Party) and its object (the masses) was the notion that the proletariat—being the revolutionary class *par excellence*—was destined to emancipate mankind in the process of liberating itself from its existence under capitalism. Save for his employment of the term "reification" (*Verdinglichung*) instead of the better known "alienation" (*Entfremdung*)—a concept which entered the public mind a decade later, when Marx's early writings became fully available—Lukács had substantially reverted to the standpoint occupied by Marx in 1844 and 1845. What constituted the originality of the youthful Marx in those days was the belief that a mere spark of critical self-awareness could ignite the revolutionary tinder heaped up by the inhuman conditions of life imposed upon the early proletariat. In enabling the oppressed to attain an adequate consciousness of their true role, critical *theory* translates itself into revolutionizing *practice*, thereby shedding its contemplative (philosophical) garb. Consciousness thus appeared in a role altogether different from that allotted to it by the scientific positivism of the later nineteenth century. So far from merely "reflecting" an ongoing process, it *transformed* the total historical situation in which it was embedded. It was able to do this because at certain privileged moments a "revolution in thought" acquired the character of a material force. In situations of this kind—revolutionary situations in the Marxian sense—the conventional distinction between theory and practice breaks down; or rather, the relationship between them is seen to be a dialectical one: they are elements (*Momente*) of a totality (history) which is suddenly, as it were, rendered transparent. The cleavage between "objective" external facts and "subjective" reasoning about them is overcome by the appearance of the "identical subject-object" of history: a fraction of mankind (the revolutionary class) raised to the level of self-awareness.[5]

In effecting this return to the position of the early Marx, Lukács departed from orthodoxy, and he compounded the offense by refusing to sanction the "materialist" view of cognition as a mirror-image (*Abbild*) of an external world radically divorced from the human mind. In all these respects he could claim to be faithful to Hegel and Marx. The category of "totality," which occupied the key role in his thinking, formed part of the idealist heritage Marx had incorporated in his own theory. The discovery that the author of *Capital* had been a humanist whose studies in economics concretized a philosophical critique of bourgeois society still lacked the confirmation it was to receive when the unpublished draft of *Capital*—the 1857–1858 *Grundrisse der Kritik*

[5] For Lukács' exposition of this theme, see *Geschichte und Klassenbewusstsein*, pp. 218 ff., 257 ff. For a critical commentary see Iring Fetscher, "Das Verhältnis des Marxismus zu Hegel," in *Marxismusstudien*, III (Tübingen, 1960), 66 ff. The preface composed by Lukács in 1967 for the republication of his work contains an apology for its excessive Hegelianism, and in particular repudiates the notion of an "identical subject-object" of history, i.e., a self-activating force shaping the world in the act of uniting theory and practice.

der Politischen Ökonomie—eventually saw the light in 1939–1941, but in the absence of documentary proof, Lukács had intuitively seen through the positivist disguise Marx deliberately assumed in his later years. All this was scandalous enough, and it accounts for the torrent of reproach that descended upon him once Moscow gave the signal. What requires some explanation is the very mixed reception his work received from Western readers who on other grounds might have been expected to sympathize with so notable a heretic.

Lukács had in fact affronted not merely the nascent Soviet orthodoxy, but also those Western Socialists who for two generations had systematically tried to gain academic respectability for Marx by representing his work as a "value-free" construction only very distantly related to its author's Hegelian origin. That the study of "facts" must be sharply distinguished from "value judgments" was a principle dear not only to natural scientists, but also to sociologists—whatever their political orientation—who aspired to professional recognition in the academic world. The philosophical basis for this rigid dissociation of "facts" from "values" had been furnished by the neo-Kantian school, which counted influential followers among liberals and Socialists alike. For the growing army of sociologists Max Weber in his last years set the tone with his stoical pessimism and his refusal to indulge in moral or religious uplift. What underlay this attitude was the conviction that, for anyone who did not believe in a deity, the truth about life was likely to be intolerable, from which it followed that one did well not to risk general utterances about the world. Such sentiments had their equivalent among scientific empiricists or Freudian psychologists, but the neo-Kantians made a point of cultivating a kind of stoicism that relegated metaphysical speculation to the attic, or rather to the nursery. Commitment to science (*Wissenschaft*) was supposed to carry an obligation to refrain from painting the universe in colors agreeable to the poet or the old-fashioned idealist philosopher. Worst of all, to their minds, was the presumption of such writers as Lukács who asserted that the built-in limitations of human cognition, or the ineradicable barrier between the scientific study of "facts" and the practical commitment to "values," could be overcome by going back to the discredited philosophy of Hegel. And when he affirmed that the seeming irrationality of existence was simply a cultural disease, a consequence of "reification" under the conditions of bourgeois society, even such Socialists as Karl Mannheim—a prominent fugitive from Budapest who later attained renown in Heidelberg with an eclectic doctrine extracted in about equal parts from Weber and Lukács—felt obliged to raise their voices in protest.

Yet it was precisely this rejection of the fact-value dichotomy that made Lukács important for an entire generation of Central European intellectuals who had outgrown the optimistic outlook of the pre-1914 era, disliked the romantic irrationalism of the Right, and had no faith in the quasi-mystical socialist utopianism of such writers as Ernst Bloch. They found in Lukács' work of 1923 what no other theorist was able to provide: a Marxist analysis which stuck to the facts and yet did *not* renounce the Hegelian inheritance in the name of "science." Until the appearance of his book, these intellectuals had regarded Communism as a mere extension of the Russian revolution: doubtless an important event, but one that did not seem to promise a solution of their own problems: a purely political movement centered on a relatively backward country. What Lukács did was to claim universal significance for it. In his interpretation of Marxism the proletarian revolution appeared as the key to the riddle of history. That so large a claim could be rendered plausible was due to more than the accidental circumstances responsible for the peculiar mental climate of the Weimar Republic. In assailing scientism and neo-Kantianism alike, Lukács struck at the very nerve-center of contemporary philosophy. If he was right, the positivist faith in science was no more than a bourgeois illusion when applied to the concrete totality known as history. An assertion of this kind could indeed also be sustained from the standpoint of the extreme Right, and indeed these were the years when Oswald Spengler, the poor man's Nietzsche, made his major impact upon the German middle class; his *Decline of the West* (1918–1922) did much to prepare this important stratum for the advent of the Third Reich. Had the German and Austrian Communists been less besotted by unquestioning loyalty to Moscow, they would have recognized in Lukács' work an effective reply to Spengler and to Heidegger, whose *Sein und Zeit* (1927) depraved the minds of an entire generation of university students. For that matter, had Lukács possessed the strength of character needed to maintain his position, instead of falling silent and eventually repudiating his earlier insights, he might have done something to erect a barrier against the mounting flood of irrationalism.

This is not to say that the doctrine set out in *History and Class Consciousness* was immune to criticism. Its political message—derived from Luxemburg as well as from Lenin—ignored the decisive circumstance that a "revolutionary proletariat," in the sense of the early Marx, is to be encountered only at a stage of development which Central Europe in the 1920s had already left behind. But whatever Lukács' inadequacy as a political theorist, he raised the debate to a level where a

Hegelianized version of Marxism was for the first time taken seriously by significant numbers of Central European intellectuals. What they here encountered was their own tradition, purged of its idealist blinkers and given a radical twist that made it a serious competitor for the attention of an intelligentsia recently disoriented by the dissolution of liberalism and the decay of religious faith. In contrast, Soviet materialism could only confirm educated Germans in their conviction that the Russians knew nothing about philosophy and were invariably fifty years behind the times.

To grasp what was at stake in those days—not just for Lukács, but for an entire civilization then about to collapse into cultural and political nihilism—it will be necessary to embark upon a brief excursion into moral philosophy. We shall then be armed for our subsequent encounter with the later Lukács (the author of, among others, *The Destruction of Reason*, probably the worst book he ever wrote, but not for this reason to be neglected).

Lukács' 1967 preface to *History and Class Consciousness* is not altogether helpful in casting light on this topic. The book, we are told

represents perhaps the most radical attempt made at the time to actualize the revolutionary [aspect of] Marx by renovating and carrying further Hegel's dialectic and his method. What made the enterprise even more timely was the simultaneous emergence, within bourgeois philosophy, of currents seeking to revive Hegel. But on the one hand these tendencies never started out from Hegel's philosophical rupture with Kant, and on the other they tended, under Dilthey's influence, to construct theoretical bridges leading from the Hegelian dialectic towards contemporary irrationalism.

This passage is followed by a brief dismissal of Karl Löwith's portrayal (in his *From Hegel to Nietzsche*) of Marx and Kierkegaard as "parallel phenomena resulting from the dissolution of Hegelianism." From all this the reader is unlikely to infer what exactly constituted Lukács' philosophical originality in 1923. The answer is that he put forward a theory of history intended to solve a *moral* problem: the relation of theory to practice.[6]

In Kant's philosophy—at any rate as interpreted by the neo-Kantians among whom the youthful Lukács had grown up—the moral life was radically divorced from theoretical cognition of the (phenomenal) world of appearances. What was morally obligatory could not be inferred from mere reasoning, for while the material world might be understood with the help of scientific logic, the moral world could not. Nature (Kant had taught) follows unalterable causal laws, whereas the individual moral life is free and self-determined. Moral decisions are reached by consulting one's conscience, whose inspired utterances—the supreme example being the "categorical imperative" of duty toward one's fellow men—receive their ultimate sanction from a transphenomenal realm inaccessible to the understanding. It follows that there can be no such thing as a theory of morals in the sense of valid perception of an objective scale of values anchored in the nature of reality. Practical (ethical and hence political) decisions cannot be deduced from any theory—true or false—about the universe. For freedom does not belong to the world of appearances and hence is not causally bound. If it were,

[6] For a concise analysis of the philosophical problems that arise for those of Marx's followers who are in the Hegelian tradition, see Eugene Kamenka, *Marxism and Ethics* (London and New York, 1969).

morality could not tell us what we *ought* to do. Hence the ultimate sanction of Kantian ethics is the "ideal"—that which *ought* to exist, but does not.

In rejecting this conclusion—after Fichte had driven it to an extreme, thereby rendering it wholly paradoxical and destroying its practical effectiveness—Hegel operated a return to what was basically an Aristotelian standpoint. There was once again a practice grounded in the perception of absolute verities concerning man and the world. Hegel's ethics (and his politics) possessed an anchorage in his philosophy of Spirit, a philosophy that raised no insuperable barrier between "is" and "ought." In "standing Hegel on his feet," Marx retained this approach, although he dispensed with Hegel's spiritualist metaphysics. A Marxist who in 1923 went back to Hegel thus had no need to concern himself with the rigid neo-Kantian distinction between fact and value, science and ethics, theory and practice. *History* took care of all that, for the understanding of history as *man's self-creation* laid bare the inmost structure of man's "being-in-the-world" (to employ a vocabulary made fashionable by Lukács' existentialist contemporaries and rivals). In *describing* the human condition, such a philosophy likewise *prescribed* the ethics proper to man.

All this was implicit—and to some extent explicit—in *History and Class Consciousness*. It was a challenge to Kantian moralism and Nietzschean immoralism alike and on this ground alone deserved to be taken seriously —as indeed it was a decade later by the neo-Marxists of the so-called "Frankfurt school" assembled around the *Zeitschrift für Sozialforschung*: principally Max Horkheimer, Theodor Adorno, Walter Benjamin, and Herbert Marcuse. Its immediate effect, however, was to split the intellectual elites of Eastern and Central European

Marxism into rival factions. For if Lukács was right, then it followed that the heritage of German idealism had to be treated in a spirit very different from that of Engels' patronizing essay on Feuerbach. It was easy enough for Communists to reject the neo-Kantian moralism which had become the philosophy of Eduard Bernstein's "revisionist" pupils among the Social Democrats. It was not so easy to dispense with a "materialist" evolutionism whose Russian counterpart had been legitimized by Lenin when he sanctioned Plekhanov's writings. And it was altogether impossible for good Leninists to follow Lukács in taking over the Hegelian heritage *en bloc.* For the point where his politics and his ethics came together was the notion of a self-activating totality whereby man's essence is brought into conformity with his existence. The "identical subject-object" (to employ Hegelian terminology) *realizes* itself in the historical process through overcoming the "alienation" (Lukács termed it "reification") imposed upon men by their self-created material circumstances, and the proletarian revolution is the act whereby this process "comes to itself" and is thus effectively brought to a close; to be succeeded by the classless society of Communism, which represents the "realization of philosophy" (another theme Lukács then had in common with his fellow heretic Karl Korsch).

Nor was this the end of the matter, for in asserting the possibility of privileged insight into the logic of history, Lukács by implication affirmed that philosophical conclusions were independent of the findings available to empirical sociologists, economists, or political theorists. When employed in defense of Marxism against critics naïvely unaware of the socially conditioned nature of their own standpoint, this kind of reasoning performed a useful polemical function. Its latent danger from the Party's standpoint disclosed itself on those occasions when Lukács felt free to pronounce that the truth about the historical situation was such-and-such. It did not greatly matter that from about 1930 onward his pronouncements were generally in tune with Soviet orthodoxy: e.g., in siding with Stalin against Trotsky or (in 1963) with Moscow against Peking.[7] His heretical utterances at the time of the Hungarian revolt in 1956 showed plainly enough that—in principle anyhow—he reserved the right to assert that the Party (even the Soviet Party) might be in error. To people brought up in a Western environment it may not seem extraordinary that a prominent theologian should feel entitled to correct the mistakes of the hierarchy, but in the Byzantine atmosphere of Muscovite Caesaro-Papism, where the political authority had for centuries laid down the law (including the spiritual law), such claims were intolerable. Once Leninism had been officialized, every departure from orthodoxy resulted automatically in exclusion from the ranks of the faithful. Lukács' unending equivocations (not to mention his dramatic recantations) were the price he paid for the privilege of continued participation in a movement whose controllers regarded him with unconcealed distrust. If on occasion he repaid them by disclosing—thirty or forty years after the event— the low esteem in which he held them, and the purely tactical significance of his "self-critical" self-abasements, it is nonetheless the case that by and large he came in the end to subscribe to tenets which in *History and Class Consciousness*, the most brilliant and influential of his writings, he had treated with the disdain they deserved.

[7] "Zur Debatte zwischen China und der Sowjetunion: Theoretisch-philosophische Bemerkungen," in: *Forum* (Vienna), Nos. 119–120 (1963); reprinted in *Georg Lukács—Schriften zur Ideologie und Politik*, pp. 681 ff.

It was his philosophy that mattered, and in renouncing it he sacrificed an element of the Hegelian tradition whose gradual loss was to make itself felt in his later work as a critic of literature.

V

Any Marxist who is at all concerned with philosophical problems necessarily starts out from the anthropocentric view of history which Marx and Engels inherited from Kant and the German Enlightenment generally: man stands at the center of the man-created world of society, and this "world" includes the sphere of art, which reflects a particular dimension of the human spirit. If the writer in question is indebted to Hegel's aesthetics, he will seek to relate the Hegelian school to the heritage of German idealism on one hand, to the Romantic movement on the other. He will then confront the awkwardness that Kant's *Critique of Judgment* paved the way for Schiller's *Aesthetic Letters,* which in turn influenced not only the youthful Hegel but also his one-time friend and later enemy Schelling, the philosopher of German Romanticism. If, like

Lukács, he regards the "objective idealism" of Hegel as a step toward the naturalism of Feuerbach and Marx, he will treat the "subjective idealism" of Kant and Schiller as an aberration from which Hegel was fortunately free. The trouble with this approach is that Hegel was in some respects close to the Romantics, whereas Kant embodied the rationalism of the German Enlightenment at its purest and most uncompromising. There is an additional difficulty: Kant, who left the scene in 1804, was quite unaffected by the conservative reaction against the French Revolution, to which the later Hegel paid reluctant tribute. Kant's idealism appeared to Marx as a typically professorial transmutation of French revolutionary activism into Germanic contemplation, but at least there was no doubt as to his commitment to the *ideals* of Rousseau and the French Revolution generally. Hegel's enthusiasm for Rousseau was considerably more muted, and his discreet endorsement of Napoleon (which he shared with Goethe) reflected a resigned acceptance of the rule of enlightened absolutism which had replaced the democratic experiment undertaken by the Jacobins. There is in Hegel's attitude toward Napoleon something that connects him with Lukács' unconcealed admiration for Stalin: the captain who weathered the storm, even if he had to butcher half the crew and most of his officers. Enlightened despotism has always made an appeal to German thinkers; in this respect at least, Lukács is in a tradition solidly anchored in the passive and contemplative outlook of the pre-1914 German *Bildungsbürgertum*.

These considerations are not extraneous to the theoretical core of our topic, for the autonomy of man, as citizen and builder of his own world, is the distinctive theme of Kant's ethics no less than his aesthetics. There is a line of thought that runs from the *Critique of Judg-*

ment, via the writings of the youthful Fichte and of Schiller, to the standpoint of the young Marx. If man is the measure of all things—and this was the central theme of Kant's aesthetics—a political order which does not respect the autonomy of man stands condemned. From this basic assumption it was only a short step to the Jacobinism of the early Fichte. It is a commonplace of German intellectual history that Fichte's short-lived radicalism was revived by those of Hegel's followers who are indifferently known as Young Hegelians or Left Hegelians. It is equally a commonplace that these thinkers, who included the youthful Marx, were in revolt against the conservative and contemplative side of Hegel's thought. But it is just this aspect of Hegel's philosophy which comes to full flower in his *Aesthetics*.[1]

Lukács' approach therefore imposes a certain handicap upon him, inasmuch as he is unable to draw out the full implications of what has been called the Promethean standpoint of Marx: his commitment to the— essentially Feuerbachian—doctrine that free, autonomous, emancipated man is both the presupposition of philosophy and the true goal of all human activity. Man is subject in a world of objects, and everything that attests to his creative power is a step toward that complete self-determination which Marx calls freedom. From the Marxian standpoint, the weakness of "subjective" idealism lay in treating this emancipation as a mere desideratum, whereas Hegel had shown that the emancipation of man is brought about in history: what is ultimately real (human freedom) comes to itself through a necessary process of conflict and self-contradiction. But this injection of a kind of logical determinism merely removed the constraint of Kantian

[1] András Horn, *Kunst und Freiheit. Eine kritische Interpretation der Hegelschen Ästhetik* (The Hague, 1969).

moralism: a moralism eternally at odds with the wretched condition of the actual world. It did not weaken what was central to all forms of German idealism—the conviction that humanity is destined to impose form and meaning upon a universe which is its own unconscious creation. Man goes to the limit of his potentialities, and while in the sphere of work he necessarily interacts with a given material environment, he is genuinely free in the realm of art. The ultimate significance of artistic creation is thus ontological: art discloses the true nature of man as a species being.

The student of Lukács' writings on aesthetics cannot fail to perceive that this anthropocentric standpoint serves him as the criterion for judging all works of art. The category of totality, which is central to Marxism in general, is of special importance for Lukács because it enables him to relate individual creations to types or genres corresponding to particular historical stages in the gradual emancipation of man from his self-imposed fetters. The analysis of "reification" in *History and Class Consciousness* takes its place within a corpus of work centered upon a philosophy of history which Lukács inherited from Feuerbach and Marx, but also from the great philosophers of German idealism: Kant, Fichte, and Hegel.

Now the trouble with this topic is that it imposes upon the interpreter of Lukács' work a procedure wholly discordant with the expectations of readers who have come to the subject by way of translations of his work in literary criticism. Much of this was composed during the Stalinist era and thus includes a fair amount of what can only be described as rubbish. A suitable example is furnished by the compilation issued in 1950 in an English translation under the title *Studies in European Realism*. Most of the writings brought together in this volume are of such banality as to defy not only crticism but even simple exposition. Composed in the late 1930s, when Lukács lived in Moscow as a barely tolerated refugee from Germany, and published in various journals dedicated to propaganda among fellow-travelers, these essays have no claim on the attention of anyone seriously concerned with either French or Russian literature: the two topics then chosen with a view to promoting Franco-Soviet cooperation in every field. The intellectual level of this confection may be gauged from the prefatory statement that the great nineteenth-century Russian critics Vissarion Belinski (1811–1848) and Alexander Herzen (1812–1870) "were the precursors of the method the culminating points of which are marked by the names of Lenin and Stalin." Similarly, a rather platitudinous essay on Hegel's aesthetics not only pays tribute to Stalin's "epoch-making" work on linguistics (a landmark, according to Lukács, in the philosophy of art), but contains the statement "Only the sharp criticism to which Lenin and Stalin subjected the entire theory of the Second International, the genius with which they applied the principles of Marxism to the era of imperialism, world wars, and proletarian revolution, made possible the further development of Marxism in the field of aesthetics."

In fairness to Lukács—then living under one of the most barbarous and murderous regimes the world has ever seen, and just barely able to keep his head above water—nothing more will be said about these dreadful exercises in party regularity. Anyone who reads Lukács' prefaces to his collected essays on the Russian realists (dated "Budapest, February 1946," and "Budapest, September 1951"), and then turns to the 1964 preface in the West German edition of the *Werke*, may judge for himself whether he was justified in concluding a few apologetic remarks about previous "tactical withdrawals in the controversies of 1949–50" with the bland observation: "If I now add to the old studies on Soviet literature a new one concerning the significance of Solzhenitsyn, this is simply a straight continuation of my earlier activity in this field." What was involved in the "controversies of 1949–50"—conducted at the peak of one of the bloodiest purges of the Stalin era, this time in Hungary—may be inferred from an essay on the subject by the ultra-Stalinist Jószef Révai—once Lukács' pupil, later his bitterest critic. For Révai, Lukács' "silence about Soviet literature" during the 1940s in Hungary was highly significant. Had he not during the 1930s criticized both "bourgeois decadence" and Soviet writing? And did this not signify that he "stood on the ground of classical bourgeois realism?" A grave accusation indeed, especially since it related back to Lukács' earlier deviations.[2]

The mere enumeration of these circumstances should be enough to dispose of the notion that it is possible to separate Lukács' work as a literary critic—or rather as a sociologist of literature—from his political and philosophical commitments. The notion of such a separation is not rendered more plausible by the fact that his Stalinist and Zhdanovist critics on occasion sought to discover traces of aestheticism even in his highly orthodox utterances of the 1930s. Thus Révai deduced from Lukács' lack of enthusiasm for Soviet literature that he

[2] Jószef Révai, "Die Lukács-Diskussion des Jahres 1949," in *Georg Lukács und der Revisionismus*. See Lukács' *Probleme des Realismus II: Der russische Realismus in der Weltliteratur*, in the *Werke*, Vol. V. *Studies in European Realism* groups essays on Balzac, Stendhal, and Zola with studies of Tolstoi, Gorki, and the nineteenth-century Russian populist critics (Belinski, Chernyshevski, and Dobrolyubov). The preface to the Hungarian edition of 1949 makes the point that only Thomas Mann among the moderns can be said to correspond to the earlier peak reached by Balzac and Tolstoi.

believed a writer did not have to be a Communist to portray reality truthfully. "This tendency towards objectivism can unfortunately be encountered all through the work of Comrade Lukács." But the real trouble, according to Révai, lay elsewhere: Lukács had never really got over his hankering for a kind of progressivism—political, philosophical, and artistic—that was "democratic" without being socialist. In other words (although this was not spelled out until Lukács himself publicly made the point during the 1956 "thaw"), he had never got over the dreadful heresy of his "Blum theses," when he tried to drag the Hungarian Communists out of their sectarian contempt for the democratic tradition:

> What is the source of these notions? [In his involvement with] the struggle against fascism, Comrade Lukács has forgotten the struggle against capitalism— not only during the past five years, but already much earlier. In his fight against imperialist decadence he attempted to confront fascism with the ancient plebeian popular-revolutionary forms and traditions of bourgeois democracy, generalizing, idealizing and mythologizing them. . . . Deeply embedded within the literary theory of Comrade Lukács, which confronts the literature of imperialist decadence, the ideology of fascism, with the great bourgeois realism, there lies concealed the idea of a return to "plebeian democracy" as a system possessing a stable character.[3]

Now oddly enough there is something in this complaint, although it needs to be phrased in less sectarian language. What Isaac Deutscher on one occasion called "Lukács' intellectual love affair" with Thomas Mann does illuminate a curious ambivalence in Lukács' atti-

[3] *Ibid.*, p. 14.

tude toward that bourgeois culture of which he was himself so notable a product. But here again the topic cannot be dissociated from Lukács' personal and political evolution since the mid-twenties.[4]

Once the storm over *History and Class Consciousness* had died down, Lukács began to appear in the guise of a fairly orthodox Marxist-Leninist who had got over his "idealist" aberrations. An appreciative study of Lenin (1924) was followed by a cautiously critical review of Bukharin's work on historical materialism (1925), and by two lengthy and learned review-essays on Lassalle (1925) and Moses Hess (1926): written in German, published in the extremely respectable *Archiv für die Geschichte des Sozialismus* (an academic publication founded before 1914 for the benefit of Socialist scholars), and unfortunately not available in translation. These writings disclosed a thorough knowledge of Socialist history, adhered strictly to the Marxist viewpoint, and contained few notions that could by any stretch be regarded as subversive in Moscow, although Bukharin's rather wooden exposition of sociology for beginners came in for some justified criticism. The most interesting of these essays, that on Moses Hess, is remarkable even today for its defense of Hegelian "realism" against the idealist "utopianism" of Fichte, and to that extent perhaps can be seen as a rearguard action in Lukács' slow retreat from the exposed position he had occupied three years earlier. It drew the reader's attention, among others, to that interesting Hegelian August von Ciesz-

---

[4] Isaac Deutscher, "Georg Lukács and 'critical realism,' " *The Listener*, November 3, 1966. See also the critical reviews on Lukács' two essay collections, *The Meaning of Contemporary Realism* and *Essays on Thomas Mann*, by Alasdair MacIntyre, "Marxist Mask and Romantic Face," *Encounter*, April 1965, and Harold Rosenberg, "The Third Dimension of Georg Lukács," *Dissent*, Autumn 1964.

kowski, made light of Feuerbach's critique of Hegel, and explained Hess's failure to work out an adequate socialist ethic in terms of his acceptance of Feuerbach's sentimental anthropology. Altogether this is one of Lukács' most original and penetrating pieces of writing, far superior to many of his subsequent utterances on philosophical topics. Like the earlier essay on Lassalle, it displays a logical stringency and a command of the subject regrettably absent from some of his later and better-known critical excursions, which ought never to have been published in the first place, let alone translated. Lukács was then forty and at the peak of his powers as a writer, the master of a terse, incisive style, and not yet condemned to the dreary task of producing hack work for semiliterate audiences. The golden age of the short-lived Weimar Republic not accidentally coincided with a spell of relative quiescence within the faction-ridden Communist movement, locally and internationally. It was a favorable moment for a theorist such as Lukács who had grasped the fact that Marxism could only impose itself on the academic world, and the national culture generally, if it measured up to the most exacting scholarly standards. The German Communist Party's subsequent collapse into ultra-leftist hysteria—a mechanical transposition of domestic Russian faction fights into Central Europe—destroyed these promising beginnings, and eventually helped to bring Hitler to power, on the wreckage of liberalism, Social Democracy, and Communism alike.

Against this background, Lukács' unwearying attempt during these and the following years to enlist Thomas Mann on the side of "progress" acquires a significance cast into sharper relief by the catastrophe of 1933. In contrast to the autodidacts who made up the effective leadership of the German Communist Party—not to mention their "theoretical" advisers who had mostly emerged from Viennese coffee-houses and inhabited a dream world of their own creation—Lukács possessed a profound understanding of German history and culture. He knew—it was to become one of his standing themes—that the German Enlightenment of the eighteenth century had been defeated by a reactionary countermovement, that the basic outlook of most educated Germans was thoroughly undemocratic, and that irrationalism was a real and present danger, threatening not merely cultural retrogression but a national disaster. He was likewise aware—another circumstance that distinguished him from the semiliterate theorists of the German CP and the Comintern—that the basic orientation of the national culture was not irrelevant to the prospects of democracy and the labor movement. The most reactionary country in Europe—a country whose national self-awareness had been formed in a war against the French Revolution—occupied the most strategic, the most dynamic, and the most highly industrialized region of the European Continent. The military defeat of 1918 rankled with all classes of the population—including the workers, who in their vast majority had supported the war, even if they did not approve imperialist aims of conquest. By comparison with its European neighbors, Germany was an industrial giant and might once more become a military one. The dominant ideology—a compound of reactionary romanticism, aggressive militarism, worship of power, and irrational hatred of anything Western, liberal, humanist, cosmopolitan, or "Jewish"—had its strongholds in the schools and universities. Whereas in France the teaching profession, from top to bottom, was predominantly on the "left" and could be won over to a humanist form of socialism, in Germany the schoolteachers formed the shock troops of nationalism and reaction. All this was perfectly obvious to anyone who had his eyes open. It had for decades been the standing complaint of respectable bourgeois democrats such as Thomas Mann's brother Heinrich, an ardent "Westerner" and Francophile. It was a commonplace among the small but influential Jewish community which in the 1920s represented what was left of German liberalism, after the bulk of its troops had defected to the Nationalists. It was plain to the Social Democrats and accounted in part for the despairing obstinacy with which they clung to the crumbling fabric of the Republic they had brought to birth in 1918. The fact that they had botched the job—and in the process lost their hold over the minority of genuinely radical workers and intellectuals—did not invalidate their perception that they were perched on top of a volcano. The Weimar Republic was not merely unpopular (after 1920 it could not even count on a reliable parliamentary majority): its mere existence evoked furious rages in the breasts of the military, most of the students, a majority of the teaching profession in the schools and universities, much of the peasantry, and the bulk of the provincial middle class. The twin pillars of the original Weimar coalition—Social Democracy and the Catholic Church—possessed no standing in the eyes of the Army, the landed gentry, or the Protestant upper class. The Social Democrats had only the trade unions to fall back on, and the Catholics—as Hitler's easy triumph in 1933 was to demonstrate—were only too ready to abandon the sinking ship and rally to an authoritarian regime.

In these circumstances there were sound short-term and long-term reasons for attempting to make socialism palatable to a middle class that had forgotten or repudiated its commitment to liberal humanism and the democratic ideals of 1848. Lukács' Stalinist opponents who in later years accused him of attempting to revive the heritage of the French Revolution were not wholly wrong. The point they missed was that in Germany there was every reason for trying to ground a commitment to Marxism in the sort of radical humanism that had once been represented by writers like Georg Büchner, Heinrich Heine, Nikolaus Lenau, or the liberal aristocrat Platen—a special favorite of Lukács. The German scene at one time—between 1830 and 1848—had featured both a radical breakthrough in thought and a humanist upsurge in poetry. Without straining the evidence unduly it could be argued that these currents related back to the great age of classical German philosophy, literature, and art: the age of Goethe, Hegel, and Beethoven. In taking his stand on this ground, and in trying to annex Thomas Mann to the humanist tradition, Lukács was not simply operating a propagandist maneuver: he was making an attempt to establish Marx and Engels as classics of German literature. His Social Democratic predecessors in this line—the Marx biographer and literary critic Franz Mehring (1846–1919) above all—had not succeeded in converting more than an insignificant fraction of the liberal middle class to the socialist cause. Lukács deliberately took up where Mehring had left off. A philosopher by training, he had no illusions as to the supposed unimportance of the "ideological superstructure." The decisive battle had to be fought out at the level of conscious choice between the two basic currents within German culture: rationalism and humanism on one hand, irrationalism and barbarism on the other. In political terms, the intelligentsia had to be converted. But this could never be achieved by dinning propaganda into its reluctant ears. The conversion had to be genuine, and it had to start from the awareness of a common purpose: the restoration of Germany's classical tradition before it was overwhelmed by the romantic flood and the latter's final catastrophic outcome: the "barbarization of antiquity" by Nietzsche and his Fascist progeny.

Unfortunately for Lukács—and not only for him—the success of the operation depended on circumstances over which he had no control, the chief of them being the mentality of the German, Austrian, and Hungarian Communists. From 1930 onward a fresh bout of sectarian fanaticism—backed up with citations from Stalin, but in reality promoted by the assorted fanatics who figured as "theoretical" inspirers of the various Central European Communist movements—laid down the doctrine that the world in general, and Germany in particular, had entered a prerevolutionary era. This demented rubbish was reinforced by the illuminating discovery that Social Democracy and Fascism were "twins"—a piece of insanity already propagated by Zinoviev in 1924 before it was taken over by Stalin and his henchmen, none of them burdened by undue familiarity with the world outside the borders of the Soviet Union. As part of this "turn to the left" (which also involved a bizarre experiment with "proletarian literature" in Russia) the German CP equipped itself with a literary journal named *Die Linkskurve* (*The Left Curve*) to which Lukács in 1931 became a contributor, after having spent a year in Moscow in 1930 and 1931 and sloughed off the remnants of his pre-Stalinist self. His contributions to *Die Linkskurve* and other German Communist journals from 1931 to 1933 make sad reading. They are the work of a man who had performed a kind of painless lobotomy upon himself, removed part of his brain, and replaced it by slogans from the Moscow Factory. The tone of these review-essays was not such as to commend their author to anyone who was not already a loyal party member. In the circumstances it is not surprising that both his earlier and later attempts to recruit Thomas Mann and other eminent German authors to the "progressive" cause were regarded by the prospective beneficiaries as purely tactical maneuvers. It was one thing to affirm that Marx and Engels stood in the tradition of Kant, Fichte, and Hegel. It was a very different matter to assert that this tradition had been inherited *en bloc* by what Lukács in 1932 described as "the proletarian-revolutionary writer" speaking on behalf of his class. And it was (to put it mildly) a notable departure from his previous standards of controversy that Lukács at the same time denounced any and every attempt to discriminate between art and propaganda as "Trotskyist." Mehring had on occasion permitted himself the candid observation that revolutionary epochs were unfavorable to the aesthetic mode of perception, since what they demanded was practical commitment and the conscious neglect of formal considerations. Writing in *Die Linkskurve* in 1932, Lukács proclaimed in the approved Stalinist manner, "Here we have already in germ the literary theory of Trotskyism"—Trotsky having in 1923 said something to the effect that while there would be a socialist culture within a future society, there could be no such thing as "proletarian" literature in contradistinction to "bourgeois" writing.[5] In 1932 this was heresy in Moscow, but a few years later it became the official standpoint—whereupon Lukács promptly changed course, abandoned the notion of proletarian literature, and replaced it by the concept of "socialist realism" which Stalin (acting on the advice of Maksim Gorki) had by then officialized.

Before entering upon this dreary topic, something

[5] See L. Trotsky, *Literature and Revolution* (Ann Arbor, 1960), pp. 184 ff.

must still be said about Lukács' intellectual love affair with Thomas Mann. This went back to his pre-1914 days in Heidelberg. Remarkably, it survived his prolonged stay in Moscow (1933–1944) and surfaced again during the post-Stalinist "thaw" after 1953. It has indeed been a constant since his earliest days as a critic.

Lukács' first encounter with Mann occurred in 1909 and took the form of a review of Mann's novel *Royal Highness*, translated into English as an appendix to a 1964 collection entitled *Essays on Thomas Mann*. The most substantial item in this collection, "In Search of Bourgeois Man," was written in 1945, in honor of Mann's seventieth birthday, and, to cite from Lukács' subsequent prefatory remarks (dated "Budapest, January 1963"), attempted "to elucidate Mann's dialectically complex attitude to the middle class, which, in my opinion, forms the social and hence personal mainspring of his entire career." Here one has to cope with the miseries of translation. "Middle class" is a misleading rendering of *Bürgertum*, an archaizing concept distantly related to, but also differing from, the more familiar term *bourgeoisie*. Germans belonging to this stratum— which created a distinctive culture in the city-states of the early sixteenth century, before being overwhelmed by the catastrophe of the religious wars and the rise of absolutism—had always seen themselves as the bearers of a particular way of life associated with values possessed by neither the nobility nor the common people. In this context the wholly untranslatable term *Bildung* does not signify "education," but rather something like intellectual and moral maturation. *Bildung* achieves its aim when the point is reached where the individual— the universe of the *Bürger* consists of individuals, a concept wholly meaningless to the landed gentry or the proletariat—is able not merely to stand on his or her own two feet economically, but has acquired secure possession of the values that make up the *Bürgertum*'s way of life. The ultimate refinement of these values is to be found in the classical Weimar culture associated with the magic names of Goethe and Schiller, but it also includes the poetry and philosophy of their Romantic critics and opponents: Hardenberg (Novalis), Friedrich Schlegel, Tieck, Chamisso, E. T. A. Hoffmann, Jean Paul, and others. Anyone not conversant with this universe of discourse is by definition *ungebildet* (uncultivated) and thus has no claim to being called a *Bürger*, even though he may possess the requisite socioeconomic standing. This does not signify that the *Bürger* must be a property owner, although ideally *Bildung und Besitz* (culture and property) go together. Galsworthy's Forsytes would have been reckoned unusually fortunate members of the *Grossbürgertum*, or patriciate. For practical purposes the *Bürger* is quite often a civil servant, university teacher, clergyman, or member of the liberal professions. What differentiates him from the *Kleinbürger*, the petty bourgeois, and even more from the ordinary people, is his style of life, which in turn centers upon "ideal values" in addition to the more familiar material ones.

All this, needless to say, has and had its counterparts elsewhere. What makes the higher reaches of German culture in the past three centuries peculiar is that their thematic unity was furnished almost exclusively by the *Bürgertum*'s problems. This was certainly not the case in other European countries. Neither Elizabethan literature nor the French culture of the *grand siècle* can be described as bourgeois, whereas *Kultur* and *Bürger* are interrelated terms. Insofar as the Germany which arose from the ashes of the Thirty Years' War (1618–1648) possessed a culture, it was that of the *Bürgertum*. The ultimate achievement of this culture was bourgeois through and through (a few aristocratic fellow travelers of the Romantic movement such as Kleist notwithstanding). Even the cult of medievalism, which devastated German literature between 1820 and 1850, was bourgeois: the courtly aristocracy much preferred eighteenth-century France to the Germanic Middle Ages, and the only German nobleman of the period who had any claim to be regarded as a major poet—August von Platen—was a Byronist and a political liberal. His neoclassical style corresponded, in a rather less impressive fashion, to that of Pushkin and the gentry-culture of nineteenth-century Russia: a society in which one was either a nobleman or a commoner, but never a *Bürger* in the German sense.

It is not surprising that Thomas Mann, the last great representative of this uniquely German class and culture, should have fascinated Lukács, who incidentally makes a rather unflattering appearance in Mann's great novel *The Magic Mountain* (1924) as the terroristic Jesuit Naphta, a sinister figure who combines faith in the Catholic Church with belief in the proletarian revolution.[6] Mann's patriotic attitude during the 1914–1918 war came as a blow to Lukács and caused an estrangement, but this did not last long. What had originally drawn them together was the heritage of what Lukács described—in a celebrated *mea culpa* pronounced in Moscow years later—as "my inclinations toward romantic anticapitalism": a tactful circumlocution in-

---

[6] MacIntyre, in his interesting and suggestive essay, notes that Lukács genuinely failed to recognize himself in this portrayal, to the point of characterizing Naphta as "the spokesman of the reactionary Fascist, antidemocratic Weltanschauung." MacIntyre, *op. cit.* It seems not to have occurred to Lukács that to a liberal-conservative patrician like Mann, Communism and Fascism might look remarkably alike.

tended to avoid any specific mention of Nietzsche. So far as personal morality went, Lukács before 1914 was a religious existentialist, steeped in the German mystics, Kierkegaard, and Dostoevski. To judge from his 1909 essay, Mann's romantic irony was not wholly to his liking, for while he credited the author of *Buddenbrooks* with a "feeling of dislocation from, and longing for, the great natural vegetative community," he also suggested that his irony "stems from the tragicomic unrealizability of the various kinds of longing as such, from the amusing tragedies of separateness and isolation that occur when such longing does come into contact with life." At the same time, Lukács was even then aware of the social situation that underlay Mann's ironic perception of the *Bürgertum* and its world: "There is in his writing that now vanishing sense of bourgeois, patrician dignity: the dignity which derives from the slow movement of solid wealth."

Given the fact that Lukács subsequently came to Marxism by way of Dilthey's and Simmel's *Lebensphilosophie*, it was inevitable that he should have searched Mann's work for evidence of dissatisfaction with the bourgeois way of life. Mann's early writings revolved around what Lukács later called "the *Tonio Kröger* problem"—that is, the relation of art to life, the subject of Mann's celebrated *novella*, which affected Lukács while still a schoolboy. The mature Lukács took his stand on a very different piece of ground: the Kantian (or Faustian) phenomenon of the world-transforming individual who has abandoned the contemplative mode of existence. At the same time his continued involvement with the theory of aesthetics made it necessary to define the significance of Mann's work in a manner that transcended the simple-minded reductionism of the sociological approach. Mann himself furnished the means of closing the gap by concluding his long career with the *Bildungsroman* bearing the evocative title *Doctor Faustus*, a display of his well-known self-irony, since his own relationship to Goethe had by then become a critical commonplace. Lukács, having discussed the Faustian theme at length in his studies on Goethe, had already by 1945 worked round to the conclusion that Mann was Goethe's legitimate successor:

> What we are offered in Thomas Mann's work is bourgeois Germany (together with genesis and antecedent paths). And of this we are offered the inner problems, deeply seized, so that while they point dialectically ahead, they do not conjure a Utopian future perspective into a present-day reality. There are not a few great realist works which are shaped in this way. I would mention only Goethe's *Wilhelm Meister* novels. However kindred Mann is to Goethe, here he is his polar opposite.[7]

This birthday tribute anticipated the publication late in 1947 of *Doctor Faustus*: that remarkable work wherein the *Bildungsroman* completed its historically determined trajectory from the restrained optimism of the mature Goethe to the philosophical resignation of Thomas Mann, working away on the Faust theme in his comfortable Californian exile during World War II. And in 1948, in an essay significantly titled "The Tragedy of Modern Art," Lukács finally came to grips with the topic. After the inevitable and by then rather hackneyed comparison ("Thomas Mann's general development runs interestingly parallel to Goethe's") he went on to draw the appropriate moral:

> It is thus the moments of destiny in bourgeois society which determine the creative path of Germany's

[7] *Essays on Thomas Mann*, pp. 13–14.

greatest bourgeois writers. Goethe's *Faust* ends with the scenes in Heaven, which are tangible because they spring from Utopian hope in a renewal and liberation of man based on economic foundations and a social morality. Mann's *Faustus* is tragic in atmosphere precisely because these foundations have been undermined and shattered.[8]

This platitudinous judgment may be contrasted with Mann's own assessment of his theme:

> The pact with the devil is an ancient Germanic temptation, and a German novel inspired by the sufferings of the past few years . . . would evidently have to take this horrifying promise for its subject. But even in the case of Faust's individual soul the Evil One is cheated in our greatest poem. Far be it from us to think that Germany has gone permanently to the devil. . . . Let us have no more of all this talk about the end of German history! Germany is not identical with the brief and sinister historical episode which bears the name of Hitler.[9]

The German patriot Thomas Mann drew upon an intuitive understanding of his people which undercut Lukács' sociological apparatus.

The contrast is all the more noteworthy in that politically there was now at last some common ground. Having become a firm adherent of liberal democracy—and an American citizen, who even expressed some distaste at the thought of having to revisit Germany—Thomas Mann after the war was as much of an "anti-Fascist" as Lukács, albeit in the Western sense of the term. Nor would he have disputed Lukács' observations on the

[8] *Ibid.*, p. 50.
[9] Thomas Mann, letter to Walter von Molo, September 7, 1945. Reprinted in *Briefe aus den Jahren*, 1937–47, p. 446.

tragedy of the German *Bürgertum*; indeed, on occasion he employed almost identical language. But the notion that what had gone wrong with Germany was simply the failure of the brief experiment with liberal democracy in 1848 struck him as curiously naïve. Mann knew his countrymen too well for that. Thus he approvingly cited Hermann Hesse to the effect that the Germans were "impossible as a political nation—I want to have nothing further to do with them." As for the notion that the "pact with the devil" had premodern roots—what could this sort of talk mean to Lukács, for whom the religious dimension had ceased to possess any significance? The reader of his studies on German literature cannot fail to be struck by his indifference to anything antedating the late eighteenth century. What passed during the Reformation—other than the brief peasant revolt of 1525, to which Lukács, following Engels, allotted disproportionate attention—seems never to have entered his consciousness. He would have done better to take his cue from Marx's manuscript notes on the subject: notably the passage where Marx contrasts the pantheist Sebastian Franck, and the "Swiss republican reformers," with the man whom he called the "stupidly fanatical" Luther (*"der dumm-fanatische Teufelsgläubige Luther"*): for good measure adding in brackets the exclamation "philistine."[10] Lukács might then have perceived that the real disaster which struck Germany in those days was not the failure of the doomed peasants' revolt, but the defeat of what contemporary historians have come to describe as "the radical Reformation."

Whether he is discussing Hegel, Goethe, Mann, the

---

[10] Marx-Engels, *Über Kunst und Literatur* (East Berlin, 1967), I, 375.

Romantics, or Nietzsche, Lukács invariably operates with a simple distinction between reason and unreason. *Goethe and his Age*—a companion volume to the essays on Mann—centers on the thesis that the eighteenth-century Enlightenment found its culmination in the Weimar culture. Any suggestion that its principal figure harbored doubts as to the values of humanism and rationalism is dismissed as part of "the reactionary Goethe legend," a heresy which "proceeds from the mechanical antithesis between reason and feeling and thereby arrives at the alleged irrationalism of German literature. . . ." The most Lukács is prepared to concede is that even the classics now and then overstepped the borders of strict logic in the direction of—the dialectic! "What it has become fashionable to designate as the irrationalism of the German Enlightenment is most often an advance toward the dialectic: an attempt to surmount the formal logic which hitherto had predominated." As for the Romantics, they are (with individual exceptions such as Heine, who stood on the political Left) condemned *en bloc* as irrationalists and precursors of that *Lebensphilosophie* of which the younger Lukács had himself been a notable representative. The real issue is a writer's commitment to the cause represented by the French Revolution, and in the teeth of all the evidence Lukács includes Goethe among those Germans who—by and large, and notwithstanding occasional regrettable backslidings—stood their ground in that great contest. He thus arrives at conclusions notably at variance with those drawn by Mann, who (as he sorrowfully notes) pays his due to the prevailing viewpoint. "In Schiller's revolutionary humanism, Mann sees something French, while he regards Goethe's humanism as typically German." It is all the fault of the academic establishment, which for a century has put the "reactionary legend" across:

> The legend reaps a richer harvest in Goethe's later development. Beginning with his alienation from public life, it arrives, through his hatred toward the French Revolution, at a Goethe who is one of the major figures of the modern irrationalist "philosophy of life" (*Lebensphilosophie*), the spiritual forefather of Schopenhauer and Nietzsche, and in addition, a literary founder of stylized anti-realism. This historical legend is so widespread and influential that one can see how it affects even progressive anti-Fascist writers.[11]

But what is one to think of a culture which allowed philosophers like Schopenhauer and Nietzsche to determine its outlook for a century? Even granted that the "reactionary legend" has no foundation in reality, (which is by no means as obvious as Lukács seems to think), how is one to account for its devastating success? To this question Lukács replies only in political terms: Germany did not undergo a bourgeois revolution in 1848, or a proletarian one in 1918. Hence the social breeding ground of its historic misfortunes—the predominance of the small-town *Spiessbürger* with his servile worship of authority—was never effectively challenged. But a nation which regularly misses whatever opportunities history offers does seem to be a rather peculiar case, perhaps even a hopeless one, at any rate from the standpoint of "revolutionary humanism." Lukács cannot quite bring himself to draw this conclusion, though on his Hegelian assumptions it seems inescapable.

[11] *Goethe and his Age*, p. 15.

Nor is he altogether convincing in his treatment of that other classic of Weimar culture, Schiller, to whose aesthetics he has devoted some interesting studies.[12] No one would gather from Lukács' observations on the subject that Schiller in 1793 thought the French Revolution had "plunged not only that unhappy people itself, but a considerable part of Europe and a whole century, back into barbarism and slavery." Nor would one infer that Schiller's view of politics (like Goethe's) represented the very essence of Weimar classicism: its fusion of aristocratic and bourgeois values. The Marxist sociologist Lukács is curiously blind to the most obvious social circumstances when they happen to interfere with his preconceptions.

Schiller's aesthetics likewise present a problem. Lukács inherited Marx's distaste for Kant's moral "idealism," which counterposed disembodied principles to the brute facts of existence. Fortunately he felt able to show that Schiller's intellectual descent from Kant did not prevent him from overstepping the narrow boundaries of Kant's wholly inadequate theory of art, thereby anticipating certain aspects of Hegel's "objective idealism," which at least had a real, albeit mystified, correlative: the self-activating process of Mind's development in history. Yet, as noted before, it was this same "objective idealism" that underlay the thinking of the youthful Schelling, later to become the arch-irrationalist among Germany's philosophers and the fountainhead of the entire Ro-

[12] For example, "Zur Ästhetik Schillers," in *Beiträge zur Geschichte der Ästhetik*. See also Schiller, *On the Aesthetic Education of Man*, ed. and tr. by Elizabeth M. Wilkinson and L. A. Willoughby (Oxford, 1967), an extremely erudite re-edition of the famous *Aesthetic Letters* of 1795 which carries a lengthy introduction that *inter alia* takes issue with Lukács' views.

mantic movement on its philosophical side. The difficulty of drawing a precise line between German Classicism and Romanticism is further attested to by the intellectual development of the young Marx. Was the author of the celebrated *Paris Manuscripts of 1844* in the tradition of Schiller or of the latter's Romantic critics when he sketched his famous vision of a form of human life in which existence and essence would coincide, work and play would intermingle, and "alienation" would come to an end? No one can say, certainly not Lukács, who has not ventured onto this potentially dangerous ground.

Let us try to pinpoint the theoretical source of the difficulty. Lukács, as we have seen, sides with rationalism against Romanticism, and within the rationalist tradition he stands with Hegel and Goethe against Kant and Schiller. Hegel had affirmed that the world is intelligible, that we can know reality as it is "in itself," and that reason attains to absolute knowledge. In philosophical parlance this constituted "objective idealism," as against the agnosticism of Kant and his successors. Yet Schiller, although a Kantian in moral philosophy, had on some points anticipated Hegel's aesthetics. Hegel's definition of beauty as *"das sinnliche Scheinen der Idee"* ("the sensuous appearance of the Idea") was in tune with Schiller's thinking rather than with the more empirical approach of Goethe, who for all his intuitive neo-Platonism avoided metaphysical speculation. For Hegel art represents an approach to (sensuous) knowledge of the absolute, the realm of essence veiled by matter. This Platonizing side of his thought, permissible in a metaphysician, had once attracted the youthful Lukács and induced him to abandon the romantic *Weltschmerz* of his student days: if the truth about the world was cognizable, there was no need to torment oneself with religious irrationalism in the Kierkegaardian manner. The mature Lukács, having become a Marxist-Leninist, still affirmed that we know the world "as it is," but the dimensions of the knowable had shrunk to the historical world of man. This manmade universe is intelligible. Beyond it lies physical nature, the proper domain of the sciences. Speculative philosophy has been abandoned. Yet Hegel's aesthetics— and therefore by implication Lukács' theory of art, insofar as he remains a Hegelian—is metaphysical through and through. To define beauty as "the sensuous appearance of the Idea" is to make a statement about the ultimate nature of reality.

This dimension of Hegel's thought does not appear in Lukács' critical writings, where he is content to operate with the Hegelian notion of the "concrete universal," the union of the general and the particular. Hence his concern with what is typical, for the type is just this representation of what is general (human) in and through what is individual and historical. When Lukács deals with the nature of artistic genre, e.g., the relation of the novel to the drama, the method comes to life, for he is then able to show that representative characters (types) possess universal significance inasmuch as they concretize a historical possibility of human nature. From Lukács' standpoint it is a trifle awkward that it should have been the great Romantics— specifically Schelling and A. W. Schlegel—who first worked out a theory of types, and that the nineteenth-century Russian realists (who are among his heroes), were thereby led to inquire into the universal significance of Don Quixote, Hamlet, Faust, and other central figures in European literature. Still, one might account for this circumstance by suggesting that Schelling's "objective idealism" was untainted by the religious irrationalism of his later years. The real difficulty for Lukács as a theorist of aesthetics—as distinct from a practitioner of sociological art history—stems from the metaphysical faith Hegel and Schelling had in common: the faith that art gives access to a supersensible realm of being. When one says that some such belief seems to underly those passages of Lukács' writings where he comes to grips with the phenomenon of artistic creation, one necessarily ventures onto dangerous ground, for a statement of this kind is not capable of proof. It has to be inferred from what is left unsaid. For what it is worth, the present author's conviction that Lukács has retained a remnant of idealist metaphysics, while wholly failing to integrate it within his critical performance, must nonetheless be affirmed.

Beyond Socialist Realism

VI

We have now reached the point where the crucial importance of Hegel's philosophy for Lukács' mature work in aesthetics no longer needs to be affirmed in general terms, but can be illustrated in detail. Unfortunately, the really illuminating examples of this kind occur for the most part in writings which have not been translated into English. The reverse is also true: those among Lukács' literary studies which have reached the Anglo-American public are notable for their lack of theoretical content. The classic case is *The Historical Novel*, originally published in Russian in 1937, translated into English twenty-five years later, and promptly hailed as a masterpiece by reviewers delighted to discover a Marxist who had actually read the entire literature of the bourgeois nineteenth century. In their enthusiasm they quite overlooked the fact that the book deals with the novel in purely historical—not to say historicist—terms. The philosopher who at his best counts among the major theorists of literature is absent, his place being taken by a sociologist who instructs his Russian readers in the cultural background of West European literature.

The essays originally collected in a volume published in East Berlin in 1956 under the title *Beiträge zur Geschichte der Ästhetik* are a different matter. Some of them at least bear on topics that are genuinely theoretical. In other words, they are important, whereas *The Historical Novel* is fundamentally trivial, even where it is not spoiled by conscious vulgarization. The essays in *Goethe and his Age* fall somewhere between the two. The chapter dealing with the correspondence between Schiller and Goethe was composed in 1934, when Lukács was already settled in Moscow, but still able to express himself in language more or less adequate to its subject matter. *Schiller's Theory of Modern Literature* (1935) falls below this level but still manages to make some interesting points about the aesthetics of Kant and Hegel. It is noteworthy that in 1935 Lukács had not altogether relinquished the "idealism" of *History and Class Consciousness*. This essay is full of passages which echo some of the basic notions of the 1923 work, albeit at a lower intellectual and stylistic level, and interspersed with sociological claptrap of the sort later made familiar by Lukács' pupil Lucien Goldmann:

> In idealist philosophy the concept of the ideal as a contrast to empirical social reality has real social roots. The situation which is basic to all human activity and which even constitutes the specific character of human labor, namely that the aim exists in the mind before its material realization, assumes a special form in capitalist society. Its decisive aspect

is the contradiction between social production and private acquisition. . . . The dialectic of the heroic self-deception necessary to the emergence of capitalist society gives a new accent to this relationship between the aim and its realization, between human claims on social reality and this reality itself.[1]

We seem to have stepped on the familiar treadmill of "socialist realism," from which no escape is possible for the unfortunate victim. But turn the page, and one discovers that the Lukács of 1923 is still carrying on a carefully circumscribed rearguard action under the watchful eye of his Stalinist overseers:

But this negation of the bourgeois ideal by an elimination of its social bases . . . does not mean that the whole question of this ideal was merely a pseudo-problem limited exclusively to the bourgeois class. In bourgeois society the dialectic of appearance and essence assumes quite special forms. The objective reality of this dialectical relationship, however, does not cease to exist in nature and society with the cessation of its particular manifestations in capitalist society. Behind the concept of the ideal in bourgeois aesthetics there is also the problem of the artistic demands for an outward form which expresses the essence in an immediate and palpable manner. This problem remains to be solved even after the disappearance of the capitalist economy and its ideological reflection in the minds of men, and it cannot be transformed into something immediately given and self-evident.[2]

Western readers notoriously have trouble persuading themselves that this appalling jargon may actually con-

[1] "Schiller's Theory of Modern Literature," in *Goethe and his Age*, p. 121.
[2] *Ibid.*, pp. 122–23.

ceal an intelligible idea, but the inmates of a nationwide prison camp are obliged to observe precautionary rules unknown elsewhere, and anyway Lukács was addressing himself to Russian intellectuals trained to read between the lines. If the dialectic of appearance and essence remains in being under socialism, this is only another way of saying that the basic problems of human existence still await a solution—precisely because what in the same passage he calls "the confusing pseudo-problems in the realm of ideology" have vanished.

What Lukács might in different circumstances have done for aesthetics may be inferred from those passages in the remarkable study *Zur Ästhetik Schillers* (1935), where he goes into the contrast between Kant's and Hegel's theory of art at some length. What he actually did can be seen in the preface to the *Werke* where the reader is informed that "materialist" aesthetics—following the dissolution of Hegel's school after 1848—reached its peak in N. G. Chernyshevski, the estimable but not very original co-founder of Russian populism. This is followed by a pronouncement which merits quotation:

Only Lenin and Stalin, and the Bolshevik Party they founded and led, were and are able to sweep away the so-called theories of revisionism in all domains of Marxism. . . . It was only during this period that Marxist aesthetics could affirm itself; for it was only during this period that the aesthetic writings of Marx and Engels were collected, and it was only then that the systematic unity of Marxist aesthetics came into view. . . . This decisive period is the subject of . . . my lecture in the Hungarian Academy of Sciences, on the occasion of the debate on Stalin's work on linguistics. . . . Stalin's work analyzes the decisive problems of aesthetics in such a fundamental manner as to enable one to perceive the mighty development which the age of Lenin and Stalin represents in the history of aesthetics.[3]

What Lukács really thought of the matter is clear enough from his lengthy essay on Chernyshevski in the same volume, where he remarks in passing that Chernyshevski in his observations on Shakespeare, misconceives the literary form of tragedy. So much for "the greatest representative of the new school" founded by Feuerbach.[4]

But Lukács' peculiar notion of what is permissible to the theorist of an organization with a claim to infallibility and omniscience—it was not for nothing that Thomas Mann portrayed him as a Jesuit—does not concern us. Let us rather consider *The Historical Novel* before turning to the related topic of his politico-philosophical pronouncements at the peak of the Stalin era: *Der junge Hegel* (1948) and *Die Zerstörung der Vernunft* (1953). It is fortunately possible to do this without troubling oneself over his moral fortitude or lack thereof. Lukács has worn many masks during his life, and he has performed acts of calculated deception, accommodation, and self-abasement remarkable even by the standards of his chosen environment. But through it all he has never departed very long or very far from his primary goal: a theory of aesthetics which would do for the new world of East European socialism what German idealism in general, and Hegel in particular, had done for the bourgeois world. If—contrary to a legend spun by his admirers—he has not become "the Marx of aesthetics," it is at least arguable that he has done for his chosen topic what Dilthey did for Kant and Hegel: he has

[3] *Beiträge zur Geschichte der Ästhetik* in *Werke*, X, 15.
[4] *Ibid.*, pp. 130, 192.

systematized a body of ideas that was once novel and revolutionary, and thus rendered it fit for academic consumption. This is not a trifling achievement, especially if one bears in mind that in dark and troubled ages it takes a scholastic training to bring newcomers up to a level where they can begin to make sense of the culture they have inherited. If it should turn out that Lukács has salvaged a few remnants of the civilization which went to wrack and ruin after 1914, his sins of omission and commission will doubtless be judged leniently by the historian.

Viewed in this light, *The Historical Novel* is a fairly respectable performance, though hardly the work of genius as which it was hailed when it appeared in English. Undistinguished in style and clearly aimed at a middle-brow public, the book does contain some interesting reflections on the basic difference between epic and drama (an ancient preoccupation of the author, going back to his pre-1914 days) and on the problem of form in general. It is only when one measures it against a genuinely theoretical study, such as *Zur Ästhetik Schillers*, that its mediocrity becomes apparent. Once more the reader must be warned not to judge Lukács by a semipopular tract composed at the height of the great Stalinist purge, studiously orthodox in tone, and addressed to a public which had to be told that Hegel lived in the age of the French Revolution. It is not Lukács' fault that British and American readers find it easier to share his rather excessive enthusiasm for Walter Scott and Fenimore Cooper than his reflections on Kant, Hegel, and Schelling. It is likewise not his fault that aesthetic *theory* (which has to be philosophical if it is to be worth anything) is not in the English-speaking world clearly distinguished from literary *criticism*: the latter necessarily employing concepts whose meaning is taken for granted. A Hegelian "theory of literature" is philosophical in a sense wholly different from what this term signifies in an empiricist culture; hence one must go to Lukács' theoretical writings if one is to discover what makes him important. *The Historical Novel* does not come within this category. It revolves around an exposition of aesthetic concepts which have the weight of philosophical reasoning behind them, but the principles are not made explicit, and to anyone who knows what Lukács at his best is capable of, the book is quite simply a bore.

It is not, on the other hand, disfigured by the sort of polemical ardor that inspired the essay collection published in 1963 under the title *The Meaning of Contemporary Realism*. Originally composed in the autumn of 1955 in the form of lecture notes, Lukács had no sooner assembled this unfortunate production than it was overtaken by Khrushchev's denunciation of Stalin, the Hungarian rising of 1956, and Lukács' own brief participation in the Nagy government. By the time he was able to write a preface to the Hungarian edition of 1957, he had come to the conclusion that while "Stalin's positive achievements" must not be forgotten, on the other hand it was necessary "to submit Stalin's own dogmatism, and that of the Stalinist period, to the most relentless criticism." This observation was capped by a brief reference to Rosa Luxemburg—not perhaps the most tactful way of reminding the reader that there had once been an age when Marxist writers did not spend their time apologizing for tyrants. The essays themselves were thoroughly Stalinist in tone and content, so much so that at last one prominent American critic of unquestionably left-wing views wondered aloud in print whether they were meant to be taken seriously.[5] Unfortunately one cannot doubt that Lukács was in earnest when he composed them, for in campaigning against various modern authors he was pursuing a line of thought which had already become habitual to him before he sank to the Zhdanovist level.

If the book had a theme, it was doctrinaire hostility to all forms of modernism: a category under which Lukács had come to include Freudian psychology, atonal music, and the works of Joyce, Proust, Beckett, and Kafka. All he could see in these writers was something he termed "subjectivism," supposedly a characteristic of "the experience of the modern bourgeois intellectual." This imputation makes no sense even in sociological terms, for the audience of such writers—in East and West alike—is no longer "bourgeois." The problems all contemporary intellectuals confront are those of a bureaucratized order whose controllers—whether they be corporation managers or political planners—share a technocratic faith in their own ability to make "the system" work: provided the citizens keep quiet, do not interfere with the mechanism, and content themselves with private gratifications. Had the Lukács of 1955, who composed these studies, still been capable of applying a Marxist analysis to the reality around him, he would have discovered that "alienation" is not confined to Western society, and that positivist scientism has its Stalinist counterpart. But in that case he would have had to renounce the Manichaean distinction between "socialism" (supposedly realized in the East European police state) and "imperialism." In short, he would have had to abandon the political credo to which he had become

[5] Harold Rosenberg, "The Third Dimension of Georg Lukács," in *Dissent*, Autumn 1964.

a voluntary convert. And there could be no question of that—not in the 1950s, anyway. *The Meaning of Contemporary Realism* was an exercise in Cold War polemics, pure and simple.

Yet even in those days it would have been a mistake to underrate Lukács' agility and his capacity for adapting to new situations. In 1955 he had felt certain that "modernism leads not only to the destruction of traditional literary forms, but to the death of literature as such"; and he had illustrated this thesis by referring to "Expressionism and Surrealism" in general, and to Joyce, Kafka, and other modernists in particular. When in 1964 he came to write a new preface for *The Historical Novel* (reprinted as volume 6 in the West German edition of the *Werke*) he had had time to think things over. He had also freed himself from part of the ideological strait jacket which for so many years had given to his writings an appearance not merely of intellectual rigidity, but of total insensitivity to the process of literary creation. Writing once more for a civilized audience, he recovered his early manner sufficiently to deliver himself of the following passage:

> The contrast between the novel of the eighteenth and that of the nineteenth century is immediately obvious. But this antithesis does not apply—or at any rate only with considerable reservations—to Swift. With him not only is there no conscious expression of the socio-historical *hic-et-nunc*: it is set aside formally. There is an entire human epoch with whose most general conflicts Man as such . . . is confronted. That is what is nowadays known as *condition humaine*, but this overlooks the fact that Swift after all does not deal with man as such, but with his fate in a historically determined society. Swift's unique genius discloses itself in the fact that his view of society prophetically

encompasses an entire epoch. In our time only Kafka furnishes something like an analogy, in that with him an entire age of inhumanity is set in motion as the counterpart of the Austrian (Bohemian-German-Jewish) individual during the closing stage of Francis Joseph's reign. Thereby his universe, which—formally, but only formally—can be interpreted as *condition humaine*, acquires a profound and shattering truthfulness, in contrast to those who, without this kind of historical background, without such a foundation and such a perspective, concentrate upon the bare, abstract—and therefore abstractly misconceived—Being of human existence, and who infallibly arrive at complete emptiness, at Nothing. This Nothing may clothe itself in existentialist or other ornaments; it nonetheless remains, in contrast to Swift and Kafka, an empty Nothing.[6]

A comparison between this passage and the relevant chapter in *The Meaning of Contemporary Realism*, where Kafka (after being unfavorably contrasted as a "bourgeois modernist" with the "bourgeois realist" Thomas Mann) was patronizingly credited with having portrayed "the diabolical character of the world of modern capitalism,"[7] suggests that Lukács had discarded some of his self-imposed fetters: an astounding achievement at the age of almost eighty. In fairness one should add that even *The Meaning of Contemporary Realism* contained some perceptive observations reminiscent of his earlier manner, e.g.:

Only "prophetic" vision, or subsequent study of a completed period, can grasp the unity underlying sharp contradictions. One would misconceive the role of perspective in literature, though, if one were to

[6] *Probleme des Realismus III*, pp. 9–10.
[7] *The Meaning of Contemporary Realism*, p. 77.

identify "prophetic" understanding with correct political foresight. If such foresight were the criterion,
there would have been no successful typology in nineteenth-century literature. For it was precisely the
greatest writers of that age—Balzac and Stendhal,
Dickens and Tolstoy—who erred most in their view
of what the future would be like.[8]

Passages such as this occur alongside polemical exercises that fall below the level of what a competent journalist such as Ehrenburg might have produced. Thus:

Earlier, I quoted Adorno's remark that modern music
had lost the original authenticity of *Angst*. This, and
similar instances, being interpreted, could well be
taken as an admission of defeat in the field of nuclear
war preparations, an admission of loss of ground in
the Cold War, as new perspectives for peace begin
to open up. Modernism, based on nihilism, is losing
that suggestive power which contrived to invest Noth-
ingness with a false objectivity. . . . Thus, as the crisis
of modernism deepens, critical realism grows in importance.[9]

This kind of unconscious self-parody had by 1955
become so much part of Lukács' habitual manner that
even his apologists began to despair of him. All the
greater was their relief when a decade later he blos-
somed out as a philosophical "coexistentialist" in every
field, literary and artistic modernism included. The
various new prefaces reprinted in the complete *Werke*
displayed a remarkable mellowness of tone, in part no
doubt attributable to age and security, but likewise reflecting the new intellectual climate in Central Europe:
a climate not wholly unfamiliar to one who remembered

[8] *Ibid.*, p. 56.
[9] *Ibid.*, p. 81.

"the closing stage of Francis Joseph's reign." An authoritarian regime—as distinct from a genuinely totalitarian one, which is dynamic and terroristic at the same time —asks nothing of its philosophers beyond a minimum of discretion. As long as they do not interfere with matters of state, they are free (within reasonable limits) to say what they like. It was thus under Metternich and under Francis Joseph, who ruled in Vienna when Lukács first spread his wings. In this respect at least, both Lukács and the culture he represents have come full circle.

An End to Reason?

vii

In the case of art it is well known that certain flourishing periods are not by any means proportionate to the general development of society, hence to its material foundation, the skeleton, as it were, of its organization. For example the Greeks as compared with the moderns, or Shakespeare. In the case of certain art forms, e.g., the epos, it is even recognized that they can never be produced in their universal epoch-making classical form once artistic production as such has begun; hence that within the artistic world certain important formations are possible only at a primitive stage of art's development. If this applies to the interrelation between the various modes within the sphere of art, it is even less surprising that it should be the case in the relationship of the entire artistic realm to the general development of society.[1]

[1] Karl Marx, *Grundrisse der Kritik der Politischen Ökonomie* (East Berlin, 1953), p. 30.

An observation such as Marx's above tells one a good deal about the Hegelian origin of his thought. It is plain that on occasion Marx envisaged the possibility of art simply coming to an end in a completely rationalized world: a prospect he viewed without enthusiasm. Thus in the passage just cited he continues:

> Greek art presupposes Greek mythology. . . . Egyptian mythology could never have become the foundation or the matrix of Greek art, but there had to be *some* mythology. Hence in any case not a social development which excludes any and every mythological, or mythologizing, relationship to nature, and thus demands from the artist an imagination independent of mythology.

Having been brought up on Hegel's *Phenomenology of Spirit*, Marx could hardly come to any other conclusion. A state of mind more profoundly stoical in its acceptance of fate and more remote from the cheerful imbecility of "socialist realism" it would be difficult to imagine.

While some contemporary Marxists, e.g., the Austrian writer Ernst Fischer, have sought refuge in the notion that artistic creation conserves an ineradicable element of primitive magic which guarantees its survival,[2] Lukács has been impeded in his mature work by his radical historicism. When taken to the extreme to which he has driven it, such an attitude makes it impossible to concede the relevance of anything describable—in his own half-contemptuous phrase—as *"condition humaine."* Yet without some such notion at the back of his

[2] "Art is necessary in order that man should be able to recognize and change the world. But art is also necessary by virtue of the magic inherent in it." Ernst Fischer, *The Necessity of Art: A Marxist Approach* (London, 1963), p. 14. For a full-scale treatment of the subject, see Arnold Hauser, *The Social History of Art* (London and New York, 1951); cf. his *Sozialgeschichte der Kunst und Literatur* (Munich, 1953).

mind, a theorist who starts from Hegel must either en-
visage the gloomy possibility with which Marx had toyed
or else postulate "an imagination independent of mythology." The 1720 pages of Lukács two-volume *magnum
opus* of 1963, *Die Eigenart des Ästhetischen*, represent
his attempt to settle the question that has haunted him
all his life.

Before trying to engage this topic we are obliged to
tackle two earlier works of his, both written and published at the peak of the Stalin era: *Der junge Hegel*
(completed in 1938 but not published until 1948) and
*Die Zerstörung der Vernunft (The Destruction of Rea-
son)* (1953). Reprinted as volumes 8 and 9 of the
Werke, they are available to anyone curious to discover
what sort of contribution their distinguished author then
made to the corpus of literature (the term seems curiously appropriate) produced in Eastern Europe during
what has officially come to be known as "the age of the
personality cult." As such Lukács' writings of this period
have a certain macabre fascination, and for the rest
they may be studied by connoisseurs of the genre as
notable exercises in the art of sinking. *Der junge Hegel*
need not detain us long. Its central thesis—that the
youthful Hegel never went through a religious phase—
has been politely ignored even by critics generally
favorable to Lukács.[3] For the rest the book contributes
little to the subject that Lukács had not himself already said earlier and in more scholarly language.

The Destruction of Reason, a tome of 750 pages,
deals polemically with the history of German philosophy
from Schelling to Heidegger and Jaspers, contains a
section on "German sociology in the imperialist period"
and one on Social Darwinism, and is graced by a lengthy

[3] See Horst Althaus, *Georg Lukács* (Bern, 1962), pp. 24–25.

preface in which "the people of Dürer and Thomas Münzer, of Goethe and Karl Marx" is urged to free itself from the shameful heritage of irrationalism, an inheritance culminating in the murderous lunacies of the Third Reich. Attempts have been made to find some merit in this inflated polemical exercise, on the grounds that German history has in fact been marked by successive disasters and that the final catastrophe was, in part at least, mediated by reactionary currents of thought operative since the so-called "war of liberation" against Napoleon in 1813. Setting aside the fact that this theme had been a commonplace of radical journalism since the 1830s (it was originally introduced by Ludwig Börne and Heinrich Heine, both, not accidentally, Jewish intellectuals self-exiled to Paris), Lukács undercut his own position by adopting Engels' thesis that Germany's national development had been fatally dislocated by the failure of the 1525 peasant revolt, coinciding as it did with the opening phase of the Protestant Reformation. For if this was so, then one had to infer that the subsequent evolution before and after the Bismarck era was predetermined. On the peculiar interpretation of "historical materialism" which Lukács shares with Engels (but not with Marx), this conclusion is unavoidable, although it is noteworthy that Engels in the 1870s tried to get around it by suggesting that the working class would bring about the democratic revolution which Germany had somehow missed in its bourgeois age (Marx was less hopeful). For the rest, a work such as *The Destruction of Reason*, in order to achieve its pedagogic purpose, would have had to dispense with the kind of political abuse which at the time of its composition still formed part of Lukács' stock-in-trade.

It is tempting to leave the matter there, but unfortunately one cannot draw a rigid dividing line between this production and Lukács two-volume treatise on aesthetics. For all its political motivation and its frequently extravagant language, *The Destruction of Reason* does have a theoretical kernel, which is why it is necessary to come to grips with it. Like the treatise on Hegel, this polemic against Schelling's heirs was, among other things, an exercise in what Lukács had by then come to regard as his principal preoccupation: the defense of "materialism" against its detractors. The term "materialism" here does not signify the naturalist humanism of the young Marx (itself a development of French eighteenth-century thought) but rather the transcript theory of cognition Lukács had come to share with Lenin. In technical language it is a form of epistemological realism. What it affirms is that human thought portrays an "objective" world independent of the mind, not one that is "constituted" by our mental apparatus. Moreover, the doctrine asserts that any departure from this standpoint leads to "subjectivism" and ultimately to madness, intellectual or political. The point was rammed home with special reference to Lenin's philosophical notebooks on Hegel, thus affording Lukács the belated satisfaction of getting even with those Communist critics who had assailed him thirty years earlier.[4]

As Lukács sees it, there is indeed a "discrepancy" between thought and its object, but it is merely relative and can be overcome with the aid of Hegel's dialectical logic. And it is precisely here that everything is at stake, for irrationalism has its ultimate source in a failure to bridge the gulf separating reality from its mental mirror-image (*Abbild*). What irrationalism asserts—and what in the end becomes a source of collective insanity—is

[4] *Die Zerstörung der Vernunft*, p. 87.

the radical separation of thinking from being. Because at every stage of human development there are theoretical problems which give rise to seemingly insoluble logical puzzles, the irrationalist concludes that the veritable nature of Being is wholly impenetrable to discursive reasoning; whereas if he possessed a secure hold upon the Hegelian dialectic of appearance and reality, he would see that the problem is not insoluble: the truth about the world is (in principle anyhow) accessible to Reason. But if this is so, then why is there such a thing as irrationalism at all, and why does it at times have the power to confuse not just individual thinkers but entire cultures? Because (according to Lukács) the task of penetrating ever deeper into the structure of reality encounters not merely theoretical but practical obstacles. Society is riven by conflict, and the social position (*Klassenlage*) of a thinker (or a school) determines the decision in favor of rationality or irrationality. Those who shrink back from *particular* insights because they cannot bear the truth will tend to believe that thought is powerless *in general*. In short, the conflict between rationalism and irrationalism is tied up with the class struggle.[5]

What does all this have to do with aesthetics? For Lukács everything turns upon the recognition of one single central truth: realism in art (like realism in philosophy) *portrays* the world, in the sense that—however complex the formal mediations employed in the process—it enables men to perceive their own true nature. Pictorial naturalism, so far from being the best means thereto, reflects only surface phenomena. "Subjectivist" modernism, on the other hand, corresponds to "subjective idealism" in philosophy, or worse still, to its

[5] *Ibid.*, pp. 88–89.

illegitimate offspring: romantic intuitionism. It is the artistic correlative of that progressive collapse into despair whose stations are marked by the names of Schelling, Kierkegaard, Nietzsche, and Dostoevski.

> Schelling is . . . objectively the direct precursor of Kierkegaard's conception of the dialectic, or rather of Kierkegaard's denial of the dialectic as an instrument for the cognition of reality. . . . It is significant that in the practical "philosophical logic" of the young Schelling an important place is occupied by analogy. . . . Thereby this first and as yet still indecisive phase of irrationalism becomes the methodological model for all the later ones: formal logic always represents the inner correlative, the formally organizing principle for every irrationalism which aspires to something more than the transformation of the entire world picture into a formless stream perceived by pure intuition. Thus Schelling's method already determines the way in which the problem is posed by Schopenhauer, later by Nietzsche, and thereafter in Dilthey's "descriptive psychology," in the phenomenological "perception of essence," in the ontology of existentialism, etc.[6]

Now for Lukács this is not simply a philosophical issue—as it would be for an ordinary Hegelian who could in principle accept this critique of the romantic school, on the understanding that irrationalism represented a regrettable aberration on the part of thinkers who, for one reason or another, had not quite grasped the point of Hegel's logic. What Lukács affirms, here and elsewhere, is that Schelling and his successors committed themselves to an "aristocratic" attitude which reserved the perception of truth to a self-appointed elite. For whereas rationalism affirms, or at any rate implies,

[6] *Ibid.*, pp. 130–31.

that veritable cognition of the world in all its fullness lies within the unaided power of reason, the irrationalists put forward a "bourgeoisified-secularized" version of religious faith: only the elect can perceive the godhead. This belief, already emphatically stated by Baader and other early German Romantics, later became the credo of Kierkegaard and his successors, and finally of Nietzsche, who supplied the intelligentsia of the "imperialist age" with a reactionary ideology which eventually spread to the middle class and underpinned its increasingly furious struggle against socialism.[7]

Lukács is enough of a Marxist to affirm that the final catastrophic outcome of this "destruction of reason" was brought about by political forces rooted in the actual circumstances of German history since the French Revolution. But since at every crucial turning point—1789, 1848, 1871, 1918, 1933—the consciousness of the participants appears as the decisive factor in determining the triumph of unreason, the reader is faced with what in the end looks like a plain—and quite undialectical—contradiction. On the one hand, the crisis of bourgeois culture affected European society as a whole; on the other hand, Germany was unique in giving birth to an irrationalist ideology that became dominant in the country's intellectual life, and led to the monstrosities of the Third Reich. It thus begins to look as though the German case was indeed a very peculiar one, for whereas on the usual Communist assumptions about "late capitalism" the whole of Europe ought to have gone Fascist, large areas of the continent remained immune. This circumstance is attributed by Lukács to the after-effects of the French Revolution (Britain hardly enters the picture). But if bourgeois democracy

---

[7] *Ibid.*, pp. 219 ff., 270 ff.

had such a profoundly regenerative impact upon Western Europe that one hundred and fifty years later its spiritual heritage provided the impetus behind the anti-Fascist resistance movement—as indeed it did—then the conclusion seems inescapable that Germany's later misfortunes were due to its rejection of the French Revolution. Now this is a perfectly tenable position, but it drives a coach and four through Lukács' rather amateurish and wholly unconvincing sociology of class conflict in what he calls the "age of imperialism." For class conflict was universal, whereas the Third Reich with its radical irrationalism was a unique phenomenon. What Lukács is really saying—although he does not seem to realize it—is that the romantic movement destroyed whatever chance nineteenth-century Germany possessed of becoming a nation in the Western sense. This happens to be the case, and it also happens to find support in his analysis of Germany's intellectual life. But he never summons up courage to state plainly that the decisive factor was the national *consciousness*. Marx did not hesitate to do so, and indeed on more than one occasion, when discussing German history, he made the point in so many words. But then Lukács is not in the least like Marx—a circumstance for which it would be foolish to blame him.

The Destruction of Reason, then, must be judged a failure in that it does not accomplish the aim its author had set himself. Lukács' defense of the Hegelian heritage against Schelling and his irrationalist progeny constitutes an important and legitimate subject. The introductory chapters devoted to this topic contain some pertinent observations on the history of the Enlightenment and the growth of a genuinely historical consciousness, already dimly perceived by Vico and Herder before Hegel worked out his philosophy of history. But Lukács' defense of this tradition against its detractors is deprived of real effectiveness by his private variant of historicism. As a philosopher he is committed to the basic rationalist principle that it lies within the power of reason to arrive at true conclusions about the world. As a "materialist" he conceives it to be his duty to remind the reader from time to time of what in one place he terms "the social conditioning of rationalism and irrationalism." The result is a hopeless theoretical muddle. If rationalism is conceived as the standpoint of whatever class happens to be revolutionary, or at least in opposition to the *status quo* (the bourgeoisie in the seventeenth and eighteenth centuries, the proletariat in the nineteenth), then the distinction between theory and ideology goes by the board. For why must it be supposed that only a "rising class" is able to sustain a realistic view of the world? The fact that a social order has been thrown on the defensive does not preclude the possibility of a disillusioned insight into the nature of the historical process. In point of fact, Marx and Engels consistently praised Balzac—a Catholic, a Royalist, and thus a reactionary—for his accurate portrayal of bourgeois society, and Lukács (in *The Historical Novel* and elsewhere) fully subscribes to this judgment. He never tires of impressing upon the reader the profundity of Balzac's insight into what he himself calls "the necessity of the historical process": a formulation that would not have made much of an appeal to Balzac, who was no philosopher and for good measure an opponent of the Saint-Simonian Socialists who did have such notions. It appears, then, that being on the wrong side politically does not necessarily cloud one's vision (Lukács' other hero in *The Historical Novel* is the Tory Walter Scott).

Yet when in *The Destruction of Reason* he comes to

the German Romantics, Lukács adopts the manner of the party propagandist who can see his opponents only as conscious or unconscious tools of "reaction." And with Nietzsche the resulting confusion is painful to witness. Nietzsche considered as a "psychologist of culture, aesthetician, and moralist" is comprehensible only as "perhaps the most brilliant and many-sided exponent of this self-awareness of decadence." His entire work is "a constant polemic against Marxism, against socialism, although it is clear that he never read a line of Marx and Engels." He possessed "an anticipatory sensibility . . . for what the parasitic intelligentsia of the imperialist age was going to need . . . [for] what sort of answers would satisfy it." Hence his unfortunate influence on "progressive writers like Heinrich and Thomas Mann or Bernard Shaw."[8] Even a veteran Marxist like Franz Mehring was misled to the point of suggesting that, for some middle-class intellectuals, Nietzsche might represent a useful transitional stage toward socialism. Nowhere does Lukács come to grips with the notion that Nietzsche's shattering impact upon an entire generation of Germans may have had something to do with the dissolution of the Protestant faith. The religious dimension simply does not seem to exist for him.

This peculiar blindness is "not accidental," to employ one of his favorite terms. Lukács had begun his career as an aestheticist whose contributions to the Budapest literary monthly *Nyugat* (*The West*) breathed a spirit of "formalism." When thereafter he began to move away from what he termed "subjectivism," he did so in the name of metaphysics, his turn toward neo-Platonism around 1910 having convinced him that works of art, in order to endure, must reflect an objective hierarchy

[8] *Ibid.*, pp. 273–78 passim.

of values. Now this kind of "objective idealism"—a preparatory step toward his later adoption of Hegel's philosophy—was certainly incompatible with Romantic vitalism, but it was likewise remote from the radical historicism of his later years. An intellectual position of this type could be defended only if it was grounded in something akin to what Platonizing philosophers have termed "intuition of essence." For the rest, it had no significance for the understanding of history: Lukács' main preoccupation as a Hegelianizing Marxist. We have already seen that socialism at first failed to satisfy him precisely because it did not respond to his metaphysical cravings. In fact Lukács in 1910 committed himself to the significant observation, "It would seem that socialism lacks that religious force capable of taking possession of man's entire soul, as was the case with primitive Christianity."[9] There was a long way from this youthful utterance to the furious polemics of the 1950s. In the interval the "religious force" he vainly sought in 1910 had taken possession of him: all the more reason for blinding himself to its perennial significance.

This having been said we may abandon *The Destruction of Reason* to the remorseless fate that attends any work whose author lacks the full courage of his convictions, and conclude our survey with a brief consideration of Lukács' *Summa*: his theory of aesthetics.

[9] "Renaissance," *Esztétikai Kultura,* 1910. Cited by István Mészarós, in *Georg Lukács: Festschrift zum 80. Geburtstag,* p. 193.

Marxism and Metaphysics

• • •

VIII

We have been dealing in the main with critical and polemical writings intended by Lukács to clear the ground for a positive and systematic exposition of his theorizing. Chronology apart, this change of purpose seems an adequate justification for treating *Die Eigenart des Ästhetischen* separately. When this work appeared in 1963 in two stout volumes (to be followed by a study of ethics which in 1969 had not yet made its appearance), Lukács was seventy-eight and plainly disposed to crown his life's work with a massive treatise on the theory of art. The calm and dispassionate mode of deliverance he chose for the occasion stood in marked contrast to his writings of the 1950s, thereby marking both an alteration in the intellectual climate and Lukács' attainment of classical status within his chosen sphere of work: a circumstance underscored by occasional citations from Goethe, whose Olympian manner had become appropriate to an exposition of aesthetic principles largely derived from the classicism of the Weimar culture. Lukács had always made a point of reminding his readers that Goethe and Hegel were contemporaries, and that Hegel (on the evidence of his own statements on the subject) owed a great deal to Goethe's work. But he had never before expounded Hegelian aesthetics in a vocabulary grounded in Weimar classicism. In 1963 he did just that—frequent citations from Marx and occasional brief lapses into Leninism notwithstanding.

A consideration of Lukács' great treatise on aesthetics must start from the candid recognition that it is wholly within the Central European tradition. Lukács rarely cites non-German writers, even when they happen to be Marxists or Hegelians. On the evidence of his *magnum opus* one might be pardoned for supposing that he had never heard of R. G. Collingwood. A few passing references to Christopher Caudwell exhaust the subject of Marxist aesthetics in the English-speaking world. Even within his own culture area he is curiously selective, e.g., in virtually ignoring the publications of the Frankfurt Institut für Sozialforschung and saying not a word about Arnold Hauser's *Social History of Art*, the work of a distinguished scholar who likewise happens to be a Marxist but who does not share Lukács' political standpoint and is consequently ignored. The same applies to the well-known literary critic Hans Mayer, a Marxist but not a Leninist, hence unmentionable. It is true that neither Hauser nor Mayer lays claim to being a philosopher. On the other hand, Lukács' Hegelianized Marxism is a very special confection and by no means the authoritative treatment of the subject his admirers have come to see in it. His exposition of Hegel's aesthetics systematically eludes what to Hegel was its central theme, namely the indissoluble union of art, philosophy, and religion. The notion of art as a revelation of supersensible reality is of course incompatible with scientific materialism, and large tracts of Lukács' first volume are devoted to the refutation of transcendentalism in every shape or form. Yet Goethe's and Hegel's procedure, by implicitly raising art to the status of revelation, had struck a blow at theology: a circumstance of which both men were well aware.[1] What later emerged in Marx and Engels as a pronounced distaste for Kant and Schiller, joined to an emphatic preference for Goethe's poetry and Hegel's philosophy, was the necessary consequence of the fact that Hegel and Goethe, in their very different ways, had secretly assimilated the then almost unmentionable philosophy of Spinoza. A critic of Lukács' erudition cannot fail to be aware of these filiations. If he resolutely ignores the topic, mentioning Spinoza only in connection with Hobbes and the French materialists of the following century, one may surmise that any departure from the rationalism of the Enlightenment appears to him as a temptation to relapse into the transcendental idealism of his own youth. He thus deprives himself of an opportunity to rid Marxian aesthetics of the utilitarianism which must infallibly attach itself to the subject if the metaphysical dimension is excluded. Then there is the awkward subject of Goethe's relationship to Schelling. Literary historians not strait-jacketed by a political party line are agreed that Goethe's dislike of Newton and his championship of the "organic" world-view, were decidedly unclassical. The youthful Goethe was a pre-Romantic; the mature Goethe

[1] See René Wellek, "The Concept of Romanticism in Literary History," in *Concepts of Criticism* (New Haven, Conn., 1963).

had affinities with Schelling, the father of Romantic *Naturphilosophie*. None of this fits the simplified picture drawn by Lukács, wherein Hegelian philosophy and "Weimar classicism" are counterposed to irrationalism and the Romantic movement. Goethe's one and only philosophical paper, written in 1784–1785, formulated what as late as 1812 he described as "the ground of his entire existence," namely to see God in nature and nature in God. This kind of Spinozist pantheism was certainly unorthodox from the theological standpoint, but it was not "materialist" either. Since Lukács cannot do without Goethe, he is silent on this topic. Similarly he has nothing to say about Hegel's pessimism concerning the fate of art in a world rendered transparent by philosophy and science—the source of Marx's previously quoted utterances on the subject.[2]

If *Die Eigenart des Ästhetischen* is nonetheless an important work, this is not on account of its formidable length, but because in a diluted form it conserves some elements of a distinctive approach already expounded by Lukács thirty years earlier in an essay on the mid-nineteenth-century German Hegelian F. T. Vischer.[3] What really matters to Lukács is the problem

[2] For Hegel's philosophy of art, see also K. Mitchells, "Zukunftsfragen der Kunst im Lichte der Hegelschen Ästhetik," in *Hegel-Jahrbuch*, 1965, pp. 142 ff.; "Aesthetic Perception and Aesthetic Qualities," in *Proceedings of the Aristotelian Society* (London, 1966); and "The Work of Art in its Social Setting and in its Aesthetic Isolation," *Journal of Aesthetics and Art Criticism*, No. XXV.

[3] "Karl Marx und Friedrich Theodor Vischer," in *Beiträge zur Geschichte der Ästhetik*. Lukács rebukes Vischer for having transmuted the aesthetic sphere into a mere product of the artist's imagination, adding significantly: "Like Hegel's other epigones, Vischer never really understood the crucial sections of Hegel's *Logic*, the dialectic of appearance and essence, the question of the objectivity of appearance, the genuine supersession of Kant."

of interpreting the creative process in terms of what he calls "reflection" (*Widerspiegelung*). Hence what he puts forward is both a history of art and a theory of aesthetics, the latter having for its theme a distinctive manner of responding to the world which is somehow different from the parallel processes encountered in everyday life, in the sphere of work (utility), in the sciences, in magic, and in religion. To Lukács these are all different modes of a primary interrelationship between man and his environment which he terms "reflection." The *Eigenart* (peculiarity) of aesthetics lies in the circumstance that, at a certain materially conditioned stage of human history, men developed a capacity for interpreting the world in terms that were no longer merely practical or magical (primitive magic being itself an aspect of everyday practicality). Unlike religion, which he groups with work and magic as an essentially unmediated combination of theory and practice, art for Lukács resembles science and philosophy, in that the artist and his public have emancipated themselves from the pressure of crude practical necessity. On the other hand, he is constrained to note that—in contrast to science, which does away with primitive anthropomorphism—art shares with religion a tendency to interpret "objective" reality in terms of images borrowed from the human personality. Hence the notorious distrust of art which one encounters in Greek philosophy from Heraclitus onward:

These philosophers regard the aesthetic principle—not without cause—as an anthropomorphic one, and since they consider the anthropomorphism of religion, myth, etc., their principal enemy, the aesthetic [sphere] is branded—quite unjustly—as an ally and instrument of anthropomorphic superstition. The difficulty of effecting an autonomy such as that achieved by philosophy and science lies in the fact that the aesthetic principle . . . does indeed possess an anthropomorphic character.[4]

Since anthropomorphism is Lukács' principal bugbear whenever he turns to the consideration of magic or religion, it is not at first sight obvious why he should protest against the unfairness of treating art as an ally of superstition. The explanation lies in his peculiar interpretation of the Hegelian-Marxian principle summed up by Gordon Childe—whom he frequently cites—in the familiar phrase "Man makes himself." Art, that is to say, is part of the process of humanization, a theme first vaguely adumbrated by Hegel in his *Phenomenology of Spirit* and subsequently given a more materialist formulation by Marx in his 1844 *Paris Manuscripts*. From this secure starting point Lukács moves on to the rather more questionable affirmation that the aesthetic mode of perception comes into being as part of the process whereby man transforms his world and himself through his own (physical and mental) labor. Art is "an emancipation from daily practice similar to . . . the emergence of the scientific form of reflection," albeit a reflection which preserves the anthropomorphic mode of perception. Only science really constitutes a radical break with anthropomorphism. On this issue Lukács sees himself in agreement with Goethe, whom he quotes to the effect that "man never realizes how anthropomorphic he is." At the same time his determination to rescue the aesthetic principle from the imputation of irrationalism leads him to a curious distinction between different kinds of anthropomorphism:

It is of the essence of the aesthetic [mode] to regard the mirror image of reality as a reflection, whereas

[4] *Die Eigenart des Ästhetischen*, I, 214.

magic and religion ascribe objective reality to their reflective system and demand belief in it. For the subsequent development this leads to the decisive difference that the aesthetic reflection constitutes itself as a closed system (the work of art), whereas every magical or religious reflection is placed in relation to a transcendent reality.[5]

On the one hand, every reflection is a representation of something real: in the case of art, man's essential nature and the unity of mankind. On the other hand, magic and religion do not represent anything real, even though they "reflect" something. Lastly, the "identity of truth and beauty" is affirmed (with express reference to Keats) as the essence of pure, unmediated aesthetic perception, but this subjective feeling (*Erlebnis*) does not intuit a self-subsisting realm of ideas or essences, as would be the case within a system of "objective idealism." There is an irreducible specificity of the aesthetic realm, ultimately grounded in the contemplative perception of truth-beauty, but these are not real entities; nor, on the other hand, are they mere words or labels for our feelings. What are they then? The answer would seem to be that they are reflections of an internal reality to which nothing external corresponds. *Comprenne qui pourra.*

One must not, however, give the impression that Lukács is primarily concerned with intimations of immortality or with the description of poetic sentiments. These topics do occur from time to time—and are then briefly discussed in a language expressive of genuine emotion—but the bulk of his work is taken up with the analysis of art as a social activity gradually arising from the matrix of primitive magic, and thereafter unfolding into ornamentation, mimesis, folk dance, ritual, and

[5] *Ibid.*, I, 382.

religious imagery, before the stage of genuine aesthetic perception is finally reached. Hundreds of pages are devoted to questions which really belong to anthropology, and it is only thereafter that the reader is introduced to aesthetic matters properly so described. Even when he goes into questions of style, synaesthesia, or the poetry of Verlaine, Lukács invariably comes back to a line of thought represented by the names Aristotle-Vico-Hegel-Marx. It is no exaggeration to say that his entire problematic as a theorist centers on the meaning of the terms "reflection" and "representation." The mimetic character of art "represents" the world "as it is," but in an anthropomorphic fashion, hence in a manner which from a scientific standpoint appears illusory. The conflict is resolved with the help of Hegel's dialectic. Mimesis "reflects" the being-in-itself (*An-sich-sein*) of the world by relating its features to man's socially conditioned and developing species-needs (*Gattungsbedürfnisse*). Thus, to take a notable example, aesthetic proportionality (also known as classical beauty) is "not only the veritable representation of essential relations grounded in objective reality, but also an elementary requirement of human existence." Aside from underpinning the rejection of romantic subjectivism and its late-bourgeois offshoot, decadent modernism, this formulation enables Lukács to affirm the "objectivity" of mimetic representation in the philosophical sense: "The anthropomorphizing basic principle of aesthetic reflection (*Widerspiegelung*) has nothing in common with mere subjectivism." Logically enough, Lukács underwrites Aristotle's procedure in the *Nicomachean Ethics*, where morality is brought into close relation with proportionality. "The methodological center of his ethics turns out to be a problem of correct proportionality."

Virtue in the Aristotelian sense defines itself as a

means between the extremes, which is not to say that it represents merely a "dead average." What centrality signifies in this context is rather the fulfillment of one's obligations:

> It would be shallow to rejoin that proportion here is simply a metaphor. It is much more than that. Where beauty is a central category of life and art, such a connection is bound to establish itself. Neither in life nor in art can beauty be grounded in aesthetic or ethical values of mere passing or relative nature: it must determine man's essential structure. If this determination is not transcendental [as with Plotinus], if it is not merely a radiance borrowed from a Beyond, then structure signifies a harmony of this-worldly relations immanent in man, pertaining to him in virtue of his humanity. . . . The relevant principle . . . in the last resort is that of proportionality. Therewith the question transcends matters of abstract form and touches upon . . . the basic interrelation of ethics and aesthetics.[6]

For Lukács (as for Chernyshevski) beauty is "a special case within aesthetics, a peculiar form of aesthetic reflection and composition, possible only under exceptionally favorable socio-historic circumstances." The model, of course, is classical antiquity, although this is not stated in so many words. At the same time Lukács rejects the particular aspect of Weimar classicism represented by Schiller's equation of art with play. To Schiller's celebrated statement "Man plays only when he is truly human, and he is truly human only when he is at play," Lukács objects that this formulation—albeit "profoundly humanist"—ignores the humanizing role of labor and thus leads to a rigid separation of art from the sphere of work. He backs this up by citing Marx

[6] *Ibid.*, I, 307–308.

("Work cannot become play, as Fourier would have it"), but does not seem to realize that if this is so, then the artistic sphere can never be effectively integrated within the process of everyday life, in which case Schiller's Edenic picture, for all its utopianism, retains its effectiveness as an implied critique of the *condition humaine*: a term of which (as we have seen) Lukács is not very fond.

A brief attempt must finally be made to clarify the status of Lukács' underlying theoretical concepts. This could not be attempted earlier, since to have done so would have meant prejudging the significance of Lukács' attempt to fuse Hegelian aesthetics with Marxian sociology. Now that the main lines of his argument have been sketched out, it should be possible to form a conclusion as to the success or failure of the enterprise. Fortunately this can be done without becoming involved in what is known as the "appreciation" of individual works of art. Anyone not himself an art historian, or literary critic, who ventures onto this ground must possess an uncommon degree of self-confidence. In this respect at least Lukács' practice deserves commendation. For all his faith in the general principles to which he adheres, he frankly declares himself incompetent, e.g., to judge the value of particular works of musical composition, beyond the most obvious generalities relating to their period character. The examples chosen to illustrate his case are for the most part taken from the drama or the novel, more rarely from epic or lyric poetry, only occasionally from painting or sculpture, and from music hardly ever. His general observations on the mimetic faculty, moreover, make it plain that he is primarily concerned with prose, thereafter with poetry, followed at a long distance by the visual arts. In the circumstances it would be unprofitable as well as presumptuous to venture beyond his principal theme: the status of "reflection" as a logical category applicable to aesthetics. (The term itself, it might be said, automatically excludes the entire range of music. Although Lukács would dispute this, it may be significant that he is virtually silent on the topic.)

The question, then, is what does "reflection" convey to Lukács that is not conveyed by its ordinary empirical meaning or by what he occasionally describes as the "photographic realism" of (late bourgeois) naturalist art and literature? For it must be borne in mind that Lukács sees himself occupying a central position, equidistant from "idealist subjectivism" on one hand and "photographic naturalism" on the other. In his own estimation at least—if not in that of his critics, who have frequently been appalled by his ready compliance with the banalities inherent in the theory and practice of "socialist realism"—he has been waging a war on two fronts: against Western decadence on one side, Soviet oversimplification on the other. If this claim is allowed to pass, one must ask what precisely distinguishes his employment of a term such as "representation" from what it is customarily taken to mean. The answer can only be found by inquiring into Hegel's aesthetics. For at *this* point Lukács' adherence to Marxism is irrelevant. In so far as Marx and Engels entertained any notions about the nature of aesthetic experience—as distinct from the sociology of culture, where of course they introduced a radically new approach—their standards were derived from Goethe and Hegel, with whom they also shared the conventional German veneration for the Greeks and for Shakespeare, coupled with a marked distaste for the classicist style of the seventeenth and eighteenth centuries. This circumstance alone should dispose of the notion that "Weimar classicism" had much in common with what was then known as the classical style in Western Europe. For all that Lukács is determined to set up a rigid barrier between Goethe-Schiller and their Romantic critics, what he terms "objective idealism"—that is to say, the belief that in the sphere of art man's spirit "comes to itself" by recovering the metaphysical dimension of the World Spirit—is present in Goethe no less than in Hegel.

What does this imply for a theory of art? On the ordinary empiricist view, the artist's mind is stored with images taken from nature or society, and these images are then arranged in accordance with his individual taste or disposition. On the classicist assumption, this ordering or arrangement of mirror-images copied from an external environment (natural or social) can only yield permanent results if it "reflects" the objective structure of reality. The artist therefore does not "create" in the strict sense: he portrays, and this remains true even if it is conceded that art is not just decoration. For what is portrayed is there to begin with, even though some labor may have gone into the extraction of what is real from what is merely apparent. But what is there need not be a "fact." Lukács, following Hegel, makes it plain that the distinction between appearance and reality, common to science and to ordinary everyday practice, is inappropriate in relation to art, where man projects his "inner" being in the shape of something usually described as "significant form." This something is not a mere "subjective" semblance or illusion, for it describes ("reflects" in his terminology) an existent objective realm shared by the artist with other men, and ultimately with mankind as a whole, whence our ability to understand our predecessors. Art as the "identical subject-object" of the aesthetic process articulates the self-consciousness of the human species. Hence the artistic imagination is productive without therefore necessarily being capricious. What it brings forth is not a private world, but an ordered whole ultimately rooted in mankind's collective experience. In this sense art "reflects" a reality, but this reality is not one of "facts"; neither is it one of mere "feelings." Art is the mirror-image of an "objective" realm of values, or in different language, it states the truth about the world.

Now if one accepts this, it is not easy to see how one can elude what Lukács describes as "objective idealism" (in contradistinction to the "subjective idealism" of Kant and his followers). In general, both Hegel and Marx operate with a theory of cognition which in the last resort goes back to Aristotle and is therefore "realist," in the sense that it postulates a "real" world accessible to reason. This approach serves well enough as a middle way between Platonic idealism and the sort of crude nominalism that treats logical concepts as mere conventional labels, denying any reality to the "universals" embedded in experience. It also disposes of the Kantian phenomenalism which leaves an unexplained residue—the "thing-in-itself"—somewhere on the outer rim of the world of appearances constituted by the human mind. But when it comes to aesthetics, these distinctions do not offer much help to a theorist who identifies "realism" with "materialism." Suppose we all agree that true insight into the nature of reality lies within the unaided power of reason. It is easy to see why such a belief may rejoice the heart of a scientist, if indeed he is capable of holding it for long. But how does it sustain a philosopher committed to what Lukács (following Engels rather than Marx) terms "materialism"? The reality of the external world present to the mind does not enter into question. What aesthetics is concerned with is rather the status of "inner" experience.

But this experience, however "real," can be termed "material" only in the sense of being related to the life of real, existing human beings. Beyond this point the term "material" ceases to signify anything within a theory of art. If we say that Man understands himself by way of aesthetic experience, we say nothing that is incompatible with "objective idealism" in the Hegelian sense, for this particular kind of self-comprehension is, after all, mediated by the human spirit.

When he describes or analyzes the process of artistic creation, Lukács shows no hesitation in recognizing all this. He makes it perfectly plain that the work of art transforms immediate experience into a peculiar realm of its own: that of aesthetic value. In this realm the distinction between intellect and the emotions is as meaningless as that between subject and object. Art contrives to represent human experience in an infinite process of form-creating and value-creating activities which together make up the sphere of aesthetics. Although he insists on describing these acts as "reflective" rather than "creative," Lukács does not deny either their autonomy or their universality, for all that they are necessarily mediated by the finite mind of the individual artist. The latter helps to create what a contemporary British Hegelian has described as "a universal and communicable world in which emotion is present, not as a comment added but as an integral element. That world is not sterilized fact; yet more surely is it not fiction. It is made of emotion and imagination, but it is objective and more real than fact because it has intrinsic value."[7] This is also the view held by Lukács. If he cannot bring himself to state it in language appropriate to the topic, this is presumably because of his commitment

---

[7] G. R. G. Mure, *Retreat from Truth* (Oxford, 1958), p. 233.

to a vocabulary that was never intended to describe anything but the world of "fact" in the scientific sense of the term. Although he affirms in so many words that this *is* not the case in the realm of art, Lukács somehow fails to convey the full meaning of what he intends; no doubt because the only terminology suitable to this theme has been pre-empted by Hegel and thus constitutes a standing temptation to relapse into the world-view of "objective idealism."

This is not to say that there can be no such thing as a Marxist theory of aesthetics: merely that the doctrinal approach associated with the name of George Lukács does not permit an unambiguous answer to the question how such a theory relates to its Hegelian ancestry. And what is true of aesthetics applies to Lukács' work in general. He has given birth to an immense corpus of writings which can be regarded as a Hegelianized version of Marxism or as a continuation of Dilthey's work in *Geistesgeschichte*: with the emphasis transferred from the self-activating role of consciousness to the unfolding of a process ultimately rooted in the dialectic of material productive forces and social relations. The ambiguity that runs through his later work may be taken to signify that—appearances to the contrary notwithstanding—he never really abandoned the Platonizing assumptions of his youth. Inasmuch as Hegel's version of "objective idealism" commits the philosopher to the recognition that all human creations are mediated by the operation of man's mind, Lukács' choice of aesthetics as his own particular domain was not accidental. For in the field of art, if perhaps nowhere else, the attempt to portray the "identical subject-object" of history stands a fair chance of being successful. Aesthetics constitutes a realm in which the rigid division between the external and the internal world, intellect and emotion, fact and value, yields to a dialectic of reality and appearance.

Whichever way one looks at it, the centrality of art in the work of George Lukács testifies to a commitment which places him within the tradition of German idealism. What lay at the heart of this movement has been clearly stated by a distinguished critic whose authority needs no political legitimation:

> There is a fundamental unity in the whole of German literature from roughly the middle of the eighteenth century to the death of Goethe. It is an attempt to create a new art different from that of the French seventeenth century; it is an attempt at a new philosophy which is neither orthodox Christianity nor the Enlightenment of the eighteenth century. This new view emphasizes the totality of man's forces, not reason alone, nor sentiment alone, but rather intuition, "intellectual intuition," imagination. It is a revival of neo-Platonism, a pantheism (whatever its concessions to orthodoxy), a monism which arrived at an identification of God and the world, soul and body, subject and object. The propounders of these ideas were always conscious of the precariousness and difficulty of these views, which frequently appeared to them only as distant ideals; hence the "unending desire" of the German romantics, the stress on evolution, on art as a groping towards the ideal.[8]

Of this metaphysical tradition the youthful Lukács became an heir, and it is this circumstance alone that lends an enduring fascination even to the least distinguished of his writings.

[8] Wellek, *op. cit.*, p. 165.

SHORT BIBLIOGRAPHY

This rather incomplete bibliography requires a word of explanation. For the student who has some German but is unwilling to tackle Lukács' entire collected works, the best introduction to his writings is provided by the two volumes of critically edited selections entitled respectively *Georg Lukács—Schriften zur Literatursoziologie* and *Georg Lukács—Schriften zur Ideologie und Politik*, both edited and introduced by Peter Ludz. English-language translations of Lukács' writings—mostly on aesthetics—are referred to in the Notes.

Georg Lukács—Festschrift zum 80. Geburtstag, edited by Frank Benseler, assembles a number of distinguished contributors, some of them (e.g., Leszek Kolakowski) representing philosophical and political standpoints not usually associated with either Hegelianism or Marxism-Leninism. A brief but illuminating biographical study may be found in Morris Watnick's article "Relativism and Class Consciousness: Georg Lukács." American students can also consult Neil McInnes' article "Lukács" in the *Encyclopedia of Philosophy* (New York, 1967) for a critical dissection of the topic. The author is a noted Australian political scientist with an interest in philosophy. A Stalinist contribution to the debate is represented by the collection *Georg Lukács und der Revisionismus*. From the conservative side, Professor

Victor Zitta has weighed in with his learned but somewhat eccentric volume *Georg Lukács' Marxism: Alienation, Dialectics, Revolution.*

Some familiarity with secondary sources has been taken for granted throughout this study. Citations from Lukács' work generally refer to writings listed below, preference being given where possible to those that have been translated into English. There exists a French translation of *Geschichte und Klassenbewusstsein*, entitled *Histoire et Conscience de Classe* (Paris: Éditions de Minuit, 1960), as well as an Italian one (Milan, 1967).

A complete bibliography of Lukács' writings in chronological order is to be found in the appendix to the *Festschrift.* This lists all his Hungarian and German publications, as well as translations of his writings into other languages, and is thus essential to the scholar, but in view of its length (seventy printed pages) it has no interest for the general reader.

Works by Lukács

"Az új Hauptmann" ("The New Hauptmann"). *Jövendö*, August 23, 1903, pp. 29–32.

"A drama formája" ("The Form of the Drama"). *Szerda*, 1906, pp. 340–43.

"Gauguin." *Huszadik század*, 1907, pp. 559–62.

"Stefan George." *Nyugat*, II, 1908, 202–211.

Die Seele und die Formen. Berlin: Fleischel, 1911. First published in Hungarian in 1910 as *A lélek és a formák (Kisérletek).*

A modern dráma fejlödésének története (The History of the Development of Modern Drama). 2 vols. Budapest: Kisfaludy Táraság, 1911.

Die Theorie des Romans: Ein geschichtsphilosophischer Versuch über die Formen der grossen Epik. Berlin: Cassirer, 1920. New ed., Neuwied: Luchterhand, 1963.

Geschichte und Klassenbewusstein. Berlin: Malik, 1923. Contains essays first published between 1919 and 1922.

"Mein Weg zu Marx." An essay written in 1933 and reprinted in *Georg Lukács zum siebzigsten Geburtstag.* East Berlin: Aufbau, 1955. Pp. 225–31.

"Znachenie *Materializma i empiriokrititsizma* dlia bol'she-vizatsii kommunisticheskikh partii" (*"The Significance of Materialism and Empiriocriticism* for the Bolshevization of Communist Parties"). *Pod znamenem marksizma*, IV (July–August 1934), 143–48.

Studies in European Realism. New York: Grosset & Dunlap, 1964. Contains essays first published in Hungarian and German between 1935 and 1939.

Goethe und seine Zeit. East Berlin: Aufbau, 1946. The English translation is by Robert Anchor, *Goethe and his Age.* London: Merlin Press, 1968.

Nietzsche és a fasizmus. Budapest: Hungaria, 1946.

The Historical Novel. London: Merlin Press, 1962. New York: Humanities Press, 1965. Parts 1 and 2 appeared in Russian in 1937 in Volumes VII, IX, and XII of *Litera-turnyikritik.*

Der junge Hegel: 'Über die Beziehungen von Dialektik und Ökonomie.' Zurich and Vienna: Europa, 1948.

Die Zerstörung der Vernunft. East Berlin: Aufbau, 1954. First published in Hungarian in 1953 as *Az esz trónfosz-tása.* A third Hungarian edition was published in 1965.

Beiträge zur Geschichte der Ästhetik. East Berlin: Aufbau, 1956. First published in Hungarian in 1953 as *Adalékok az esztétika történetéhez.*

The Meaning of Contemporary Realism. London: Merlin Press, 1963. First published in German in 1958 as *Zur Gegenwartsbedeutung des kritischen Realismus.*

Georg Lukács—Schriften zur Literatursoziologie. Peter Ludz, ed. Neuwied: Luchterhand, 1961.

Georg Lukács—Schriften zur Ideologie und Politik. Peter Ludz, ed. Neuwied: Luchterhand, 1967.

Werke. Neuweid: Luchterhand, 1963– . A projected twelve-volume edition. Vols. II and V–XII had appeared by 1969.

Supplementary Reading

Adorno, T. W. "Erpresste Versöhnung: Zu Georg Lukács 'Wider den missverstandenen Realismus,'" in *Noten zur Literatur*, II, 162–87. Frankfurt am Main: Suhrkamp, 1963. First published in *Der Monat*, XI (1961).

Borkenau, Franz. *The Communist International.* London: Faber and Faber, 1938.

Fetscher, Iring. *Karl Marx und der Marxismus*. Munich: Piper, 1967.

Korsch, Karl. *Marxismus und Philosophie*. Leipzig: Hirschfeld, 1923.

Georg Lukács und der Revisionismus: Eine Sammlung von Aufsätzen. H. Koch, ed. East Berlin: Aufbau, 1960.

Georg Lukács zum siebzigsten Geburtstag. East Berlin: Aufbau, 1955.

Georg Lukács zum achtzigsten Geburtstag. Frank Benseler, ed. Neuwied: Luchterhand, 1965.

Habermas, Jürgen. *Theorie und Praxis*. Neuwied: Luchterhand, 1963.

Révai, József. *Literarische Studien*. Berlin: Dietz, 1956. First published in Hungarian in 1950 as *Irodalmi tamulmányok*.

———. *La littérature et la démocratie populaire: À propos de Georg Lukács*. Paris: Les Éditions de la Nouvelle Critique, 1951.

Tökés, Rudolf L. *Béla Kun and the Hungarian Soviet Republic*. New York: Frederick A. Praeger, for the Hoover Institution, Stanford University, 1967.

Watnick, Morris. "Relativism and Class Consciousness: Georg Lukács," in Leopold Labedz (ed.), *Revisionism: Essays on the History of Marxist Ideas*. New York: Frederick A. Praeger, 1962.

Zitta, Victor. *Georg Lukács' Marxism: Alienation, Dialectics, Revolution. A Study in Utopia and Ideology*. The Hague: Martinus Nijhoff, 1961.

INDEX